Lessons I've Learned

Also by Davina McCall

Davina's 5 Weeks to Sugar-Free

Davina's Smart Carbs

Lessons I've Learned

DAVINA McCALL

ORION
SPRING

First published in Great Britain in 2016
by Orion Spring
an imprint of The Orion Publishing Group Ltd,
Carmelite House, 50 Victoria Embankment
London EC4Y 0DZ

An Hachette UK company

3 5 7 9 10 8 6 4

The author is grateful for permission to reprint
an excerpt from *Spiritual Midwifery* – 4th Edition,
Ina May Gaskin, Book Publishing Co., 2002

Thanks also to www.JohnnyBoylan.co.uk

A CIP catalogue record for this book
is available from the British Library.

Hardback ISBN 978 1 4091 6569 9
Trade Paperback ISBN 978 1 4091 6570 5

Printed and bound by CPI Group (UK) Ltd, Croydon, CR0 4YY

www.orionbooks.co.uk

ORION
SPRING

This book is for Holly, Tilly and Chester

Contents

Helloo . . .
   I'm me . . .
   A work in progress.

And I really believe this to be true: I am learning every day. I learn from every situation. Every person I meet. Every place I go.

Sometimes I am unwilling at the time to see it . . . Maybe the lesson hurt or embarrassed me, and it's only with hindsight I can feel how much it taught me. At other times I am desperate to learn. I may be stuck in some emotional rut or a parenting quandary or a self-esteem collapse and turn to friends, psychologists, hypnotists, 12-step fellowships, councillors – ANYONE – to please teach me something – ANYTHING – to take me away from how I am feeling!

Most often I learn that I have to sit with those feelings and the lesson comes after.

Anyhoo … you get the gist. I make the mistakes so you don't have to!

Writing this book was easy, like an outpouring. I didn't write it as a way of making myself feel good, but as a way to help other people feel good. Lots of people have helped me learn along the way, and I think good news or great tips should be shared!

This book is for everyone, including my own children and future grandchildren, so that they know where the lessons I talk about come from. I wish my granny had written a book like this for me, because she's taught me so many lessons in life that she learned from some wonderful people, but I will never know who they were or what the story was behind them. With my granny being so elderly now, I think about all the things she hasn't told me, and how sad I feel about that.

So in this book I get to tell you some of the life lessons I've learned and also tell you a little bit about me …

BIIIIIIIG HUUUUUUUUUUUUUUUUGS
oxoxoxoxoxo Me

Lessons from Childhood

Look after the people you love
and keep them close

My childhood's quite complicated, so just bear with.

My mum met my dad when they were both really young, in their early twenties, on a boat going from France to England. My dad had been on a business trip and they sat in the corridor all night talking and that was it. It was mad, passionate young love.

My mum, Flo, (her name was Florence but no one called her that) moved to London to be with Andrew, my dad, and got a job in Knightsbridge, at Yves Saint Laurent. She was from Paris and extraordinarily glamorous, with great style, and stick thin. She confessed to me later that she had been anorexic. That was the late sixties/early seventies, and everybody was unhealthily thin. Her and my dad made a pretty amazing couple. My dad was super-duper handsome, and still is in my book, but, sadly for their marriage, my mum was incapable of monogamy until much later in life when she met her fourth and final husband, Henry, in her fifties.

Mum was a total wild child. She'd already had a little girl when she was a teenager herself: that was Caroline, my big sister. Mum was sixteen when she gave birth but fifteen when she got pregnant, so when she met my dad she'd lived a wild and crazy life already.

There was something really intoxicating about my mother. Everybody felt it, even my granny Pippy, Dad's mum, who always had a soft spot for my mum despite the fact she treated Dad really badly and absolutely destroyed him emotionally. My mum was eclectic, naughty, impish, funny, irreverent and captivating. For example, a very early memory I have of her, I guess I was about five, is of her driving across a cricket pitch in a Rolls-Royce. I am in the back playing with the windows. Mum's at the wheel. And she's drunk. The game is in full swing and the cricketers are up in arms until they realise that there's this very, very beautiful, smoking-hot French chick in the Rolls-Royce. They go from shouting to asking, 'Who is that . . .?' I've got no idea why we were driving across a cricket pitch, but it's a vivid memory.

My earliest memory is also of my mum. When I was three, nearly four, my mum and a man I didn't know took me to my granny Pippy's house.

'I'm going skiing, Nanou,' she said, in English but with a

strong French accent. My mum always called me Nanou, short for Anoushka, because that is what she had wanted to call me. We were in the boot room of Pippy's house, the light was quite dim, and there was another man there who wasn't my dad. I remember the musty smell of the little room and the fact that it didn't seem weird that she was going.

'I'll be back in two weeks,' she said. I remember being dropped off in that little room, no loitering, no long goodbye, the kind of thing you do when you don't want your toddler to cry on the first day at school. You don't let them cling on to your leg for ever, you do a cut and run. I don't remember kissing. I don't remember tears. I just remember her going. The next thing I know my granny was shepherding me into the kitchen, there was the smell of cooking, and that was that. She was gone.

The next thing I remember is wondering when my mum was coming back. I was sure somebody had said she was coming back, but she still hadn't. I had no concept of time and even now I don't know how long it took for me to start worrying that I had overstayed my welcome. I didn't want to upset Pippy by asking when Mum was coming back, but I felt bad about still being there.

She didn't come back in two weeks. I never lived with her again.

At the time, no one explained anything to me. I had no idea I would be living permanently with my granny, it just happened. It was much later that I learned my mum had left my dad for another man, and that there was a court case to decide where I would live after my parents divorced. My dad won, which in those days was pretty unheard of. He was living in London, though, and couldn't have me because his job didn't pay him enough to get a nanny, but he felt very strongly that I should stay in England and not go to live with my mum's parents in Paris. Mum had a pretty bad track record to be honest. She had a problem with drink and drugs and had already left her first daughter with her parents in Paris. So that, and the fact I'd been brought up in the UK and didn't speak French, made the court feel it was right for me to stay with my paternal grandparents, Pippy and Mickey. In retrospect, my sister had a tough time growing up around our mum in Paris, so the court made the right decision. Being here in the UK was far and away the safest and most stable place for me to be. I wish I had been told at the time that my mum was not coming back, but that Pippy and my dad had fought to keep me in the UK and that they desperately wanted me.

My mum was so young when she left me at Pippy's house that day, not even twenty-six. It must have been very painful to leave, at least that's how I perceive it now. In my teenage years, when everything was difficult, on the days I thought that the world was conspiring against me, I felt like my mum dumped me. I was angry.

Since I've had children myself, I've understood that sometimes you do things that you think are right at the time, but twenty years down the line your kids tell you it really messed them up! So I'm a lot softer on my mum now than I was when I was younger. I don't think she found it easy leaving me.

She didn't just say, 'Well, you have her.' She fought for me in court and, after she lost the case, she probably thought she was doing the best thing for me, leaving with no fuss. I was very young, perhaps she hoped I wouldn't remember it, but of course you're going to remember that your own mother hasn't come back, and for a long time that was all I wanted. I wanted her to come back.

Luckily, my granny Pippy is a tour de force. She's an amazing woman and she took me in and nurtured me. She didn't make a fuss about my mum not being there; in fact, she almost never spoke about it. In those days if something bad happened, most people believed that it would just sort of go away if they didn't talk about it. Pippy's still like that now. In her generation, nobody talked about feelings. 'Buck up and just get on with it' was her mantra.

'When is Mummy coming back?' I would ask.

'Well, she's not coming back for a bit, so let's just get on. Why don't you help me do the washing-up?' Pippy would say. I remember it was something I could never quite get a straight answer to, and children are brilliant at being sidetracked so I'd get sidetracked the whole time.

It's not that she wasn't affectionate – I got lots of love and cuddles and was constantly told that I was loved, and she was always cooking me amazing food. Pippy told me that a psychic had once predicted that she would have four children. She only had three, my dad, my Uncle Simon and my Auntie Sheena, so she called me her 'number four', which I loved.

We lived in a beautiful Victorian house in Surrey, with a

barn and some stables. I had a vegetable patch, a flower garden, there was a pond and a swimming pool, and my grandpa taught me to swim at three years old and later to dive. My great-granny, Mickey's mother, also lived there, in a granny flat; my Uncle Simon used to come down all the time with his wife, Niamh, and their daughter, Alice; and my Auntie Sheena was still living there too. Sheena was Pippy's youngest child. She was about twenty when I arrived, and she helped my grand-parents to look after me. I loved her. She was so exciting and glamorous, with beautiful, long black hair and a crazy, Bohemian lifestyle. A lot of really groovy rock 'n' roll people were always wafting around Sheena. I think I remember playing bongos with T. Rex. My dad came every weekend too, and quite soon he met and married Gaby, my stepmum.

So it was a big, busy, chaotic house, everybody was always coming and going, and at the heart of it was Pippy.

Pippy would always be the one who had the lunch party or the dinner party to celebrate a birthday or the birth of a child or a wake after a funeral, and all the family would always be at Pippy's. It was like that TV programme *Brothers and Sisters* with Sally Field – that was my granny. She kept us all together and made us see each other all the time and that's why we're such a close family. It's perhaps the most important lesson I learned from Pippy:

Look after the people you love and keep them close.

Pippy was the matriarch and she kept the family close. When there was all this chaos happening in the other half of my life, the French half, it was a wonderful relief to come back to less flamboyance, a lot less money, less grandeur, because the thing that really mattered for Pippy was the family. I got real comfort, roots and warmth from having the family around me. It made me feel safe. So having all the family around me now creates the same feeling. And I know it creates the same for my kids. They feel really grounded when all the family's there. They love it.

Now I've lost my mum and my big sister, and my little sister lives in Australia, but I'm very, very, very close to my three cousins, Auntie Sheena's children, and that means a great deal to me. My granny Pippy lives near us and so my kids have their great-granny in their lives just as I did. My sister also lived with us until she died. If you don't have a family yourself, which lots of people don't, you can create a family out of the very best friends you have. People who have known you a very long time are extremely precious.

Never cry wolf

My dad and stepmum, Gaby, used to visit me at Pippy's every weekend. My dad met Gaby quite soon after my mum left, and I can hardly remember a time without her. Their visits became my greatest treat. I would get into bed with them every morning when they were there: first with dad, then with Gaby, because the guest bedroom had twin beds. So old-fashioned. I just **loved** having them there.

As I got a bit older, Gaby became a sort of style guru for me. I got to an age when I didn't want to wear hand-me-downs from an older girl Pippy knew, and Pippy didn't really understand that I wanted to develop my own style. Gaby did, and I began to realise that she was this beautiful, young, hip, trendy woman who knew what Top Shop was. It was really exciting! I remember being in the bath and making her sit on the loo (with the seat down, obvs) and asking her millions of questions about the facts of life and about periods and everything, and she was *brilliant* because she was very matter-of-fact, way ahead of her time in terms of teaching me all that vital stuff without being embarrassed. I had no fear that she might ridicule me or laugh at me.

I used to enjoy my dad and Gaby's visits so much that I began to dread Sunday nights on Sunday morning. My dad would have their bag packed and ready by the door on Sunday morning, and I'd feel sad all day. (I've never quite rid myself of a dislike of 'Sunday bags'. There was a dreadful period of six years when my sister Caroline stayed in London after Matthew and I moved to the country. It was the worst six years of our married life. She used to visit us at weekends and on Sunday mornings she'd brush her teeth, pack up her stuff in her red bag, and put it by the door. I'd end up hiding it, because I couldn't bear walking past the front door the whole of Sunday, knowing that she was going. I hated it. I still hate goodbyes on a Sunday.) As evening approached I would start getting a tummy ache or a headache, some pain somewhere that needed a little bit of extra attention from Gaby and Daddy. This would happen every Sunday.

Then, one Sunday, they'd taken me to see my granny-in-law, Gaby's mum, and I'd come back home and was a bit down. Pippy knew I was always a bit down on Sunday evenings so she'd made my favourite meal that night which, back in those days, was boiled ham and parsley sauce. She always home-made everything and it was always so good, but that evening I genuinely had a sore tummy.

'Pippy, I don't feel very well.'

'Now, come on, I know what you're doing. You can't pull the wool over my eyes. Just eat the food. Come on, I've made this specially. It's your favourite meal.'

'No, Pippy, I really, really am feeling ill.'

'Don't start this. Come on. I know what you're doing. You do this every Sunday so just eat the food.'

I force-fed myself as much as I could, feeling really ill, and then I went to bed. I was crying because my tummy hurt so much.

'Look, we've really got to go,' said Dad, and I could tell that he and Gaby felt bad because, by this point, I was sobbing from the pain.

'Come on, seriously, you've got to stop it. Pull yourself together,' Pippy said.

I remember thinking so clearly, 'None of them believe me because I do this every weekend. What am I going to do because I really am in agony?' And I started chewing the corner of my duvet. I remember Pippy had to re-sew all the corners of my pillows and my duvet because I chewed the corners off that night. I was in so much pain.

'I'm calling the doctor. I'm going to call him right now!' Pippy eventually said, trying to shock me out of it. 'Are you really, honestly in pain? If you are honestly, *honestly* in pain, I'll call him.'

'Yes!' I cried.

'I'm going to call the doctor then,' she said, but more as a threat, to make sure I was really telling the truth.

'Call the doctor, please!'

'Okay. I'm calling the doctor now. I'm on the phone to the doctor. Calling the doctor.'

'Yes, phone him!'

So finally she really did call him, and the doctor came after what felt like for ever, by which point I was howling and had thrown up all the boiled ham and parsley sauce. Dad had stayed, as he could see it was pretty bad.

'We need to get her to the hospital. It's appendicitis,' the doctor said.

Dad drove us. Pippy was in tears the whole way. I was rushed into emergency surgery and had my appendix taken out.

'That was kind of my fault,' I remember thinking, as soon as I woke up after the op.

So don't cry wolf, ever. You never know when you'll need to cry for real. But it was worth having my appendix out because I got my dad for an extra night. Yay! Result!

Funnily enough, I have done just what Pippy did with my own kids. The other day, Chester was saying, 'I don't feel very well.'

'You'll be fine when you get to school,' I replied. It was a Monday morning so I thought he was just reluctant to go. To be honest, he has cried wolf a few times himself.

'Mummy, I'm really not feeling well …' he said as we drove to school.

'You're absolutely fine. In you go.'

An hour later I got a phone call.

'Mrs Robertson? Chester's just thrown up everywhere.'

'Oh no, I'm so sorry!'

And when I went to pick him up, Chester said, 'Ha! Told you!' and it took me right back to the day I had my appendix out.

Will I regret this?

In 2012, I was asked to run the Olympic torch on the day before it went into the Olympic Park. Obviously, this was a massive honour. I was so excited about the Olympics being held in the UK; it was probably never going to happen again in my lifetime. But when my sister Caroline got sick it was a no-brainer: she and I would watch the torch going into the stadium on the TV together. Five days after that, she died. Do I regret not running the torch? No, not one tiny bit.

Sometimes decisions like that are harder. This might be a

difficult lesson for some people to swallow but it's one that has served me well. No one taught me it; I learned it through my endlessly difficult relationship with my mother.

I believe that my mother loved me and thought I was hilarious, a bit mad and quite funny, and I really loved her and thought she was incredibly glamorous and beautiful, but our relationship *really confused me*. I never knew where I stood with her, and as any child of an alcoholic will tell you, you adapt yourself constantly to their moods to keep the peace. So I became expert at reading situations and adapting myself (I've used that a lot in my work), but it was hard.

It wasn't that long after she left me at Pippy's that I went out to France to visit my mum for a week or so. From the age of four, I would visit her during the long school holidays, for a week or two, two or three times a year. I would fly as an unaccompanied minor with my passport round my little neck.

I was always terrified there would be no one there to pick me up. It happened a few times that I was forgotten at the airport and – high-class problem – I also used to get forgotten daily at ski school. I remember perfectly the ski instructor's sigh of anger when he realised that he'd have to take me back to his house *again*. I'd be there several hours before Mum remembered me. This all meant I couldn't trust her even from an early age and that never got better.

There were other really sad times when my mum cancelled my visits at the last minute.

'I'm going to take you to Spain,' she said once. My bag was

packed and by the door the day before I was due to fly out. She phoned that evening and spoke to Pippy.

'Actually, I haven't got any childcare. She can't come.' My mum explained that she might want to go out clubbing and she wouldn't know what to do with me. I was probably eleven then.

Those early visits set a precedent for the rest of my life. I would leave the safe, dependable routines of Pippy's house, and enter the chaos that was my mum's life. My mum was always a bit all over the place, emotionally and geographically, depending on who she was with at the time, and so I was a bit all over the place too.

Throughout my teenage years, I was confused by my mum. In part I hero-worshipped her for being so cool and free, but I was also angry and hurt. I thought she didn't care that I'd stayed in England, but I think she probably cared a lot, and the heartache of losing a child can't have helped her drink and drugs problem.

I don't want to diss my mum. She was an amazingly vibrant woman, incredibly exciting and fun, but you never quite knew what was going to happen with her, which is hard if you're her kid. I remember once, when I was in my teens, meeting my mum in a bar. She was wearing an electric-blue fur coat, a pair of shoes and nothing else. She kept flashing people and thought it was really funny, but obviously, for me as her daughter, it was excruciatingly embarrassing.

She was extremely sexual, and would flirt with men and talk about sex non-stop, to the point where I'd be like, 'Oh, please . . . Enough already.' People generally thought that was thrilling and intoxicating, but I was always very embarrassed.

When I was in Paris, there were no rules and no boundaries. I had no curfew. I could stay out all night. I could do whatever I wanted and wear what I wanted. At one level, I thought that was fantastic and that she was the dream mother. As I've got older, I've realised that was pretty destructive. I ended up in situations with her where I pretended I was really cool but I felt deeply uncomfortable, even frightened.

'Nanou, do you want to come shopping with me?' she asked one time, when I was thirteen.

'Yes, I'll come,' I said, half excited and half terrified. Whenever I went out with my mum, something always happened. She drove really fast and never let me wear seatbelts because she considered seatbelts an insult to her driving. One-way streets were a challenge, or an opportunity to her, and she would park **absolutely anywhere**. Her grandfather had been the prefect of police for the whole of France, so any trouble she got into she'd just wiggle her way out of by saying her grandfather was Célestin Hennion and she'd always get away with it. A guy pinched her bum once and she got him arrested. We were in a café and she was drunk. She went outside, found a policeman, mentioned her grandfather's name, and the guy was arrested for pinching her bum! So when my mum asked me if I wanted to go somewhere with her, I'd say yes and be quite excited, but I'd also think, 'Oh my God, where are we going? What will go wrong?'

Anyway, on this particular shopping trip we went by bus to

the Rue Saint-Denis, which is a red-light district that's cool and trendy now, a bit like Soho, but back then it was really seedy.

'We will go to a sex shop,' she said. I couldn't believe how cool that made me, going to sex shops at thirteen.

'Come in?' she said when we got there.

'No, no, it's fine, I'll wait out here,' I said, suddenly terribly self-conscious. She went in to buy a sex toy. Nothing wrong with that, I'm all for experimenting with sex, but I wouldn't take my thirteen-year-old daughter with me.

There I was, between a rock and a hard place. I didn't want to go in, but the Rue Saint-Denis was just as bad. I was barely a teenager, wearing really high heels (I seem to remember they were white stilettos), a white rah-rah skirt and a white vest. It was the eighties, and I thought I was Debbie Harry, with my hair all spiky. I was already smoking. She let me smoke at thirteen. So I stayed outside and had a cigarette. A thirteen-year-old dressed like Lolita, smoking a cigarette outside a sex shop. Guys were staring at me, people were muttering. I just wanted to cry. What I thought would be really cool turned into an absolute nightmare. I wanted the earth to swallow me up. I wanted to disappear.

It's not that I didn't love my mum. I really loved my mum. There was something exciting and magical about her, but when I look back there was also something a bit sad. She cut a very tragic figure and I never really knew how to behave around her.

Anyway, my mum came out triumphant with a bag of stuff, and we got on the bus to go home. She was always, throughout my teens, a little bit out of it on some kind of a pill or drink, whatever the time of day. She had few inhibitions anyway, but when she was a bit out of it she had none.

'Come on, let's put the batteries in!' she said, pulling out the vibrator. I was mortified. I couldn't look up. I couldn't laugh. I didn't know what to do or where to look with all those passengers on the bus staring at us. I think my mum was used to being with my big sister, who was nineteen or twenty at this point, and she thought she could do the same things with me that she did with Caroline, but I was dying. I'd been brought up in the Surrey countryside by my granny and my granddad. I went to church every Sunday. I was square and very straight inside, however much I pretended to be grown up and cool. With my granny there was order and routine, rules and standards, safety and nurturing. With my mother there were never any rules at all. So I lived this weird life, where I'd go from church-going, choir-singing, goody two-shoes in England, to cigarette-smoking Lolita in Paris.

I think if you really understand <u>that</u> aspect of me, then you understand <u>me</u>, because I am <u>both</u> of those people.

There is a part of me that still wants to be really naughty, to dress inappropriately, and do something that will horrify people. That really excites me. But at the same time I will not cross the road outside the cinema without going to the pedestrian crossing in case a car drives down there for the first time in ten years. Half of me is the result of Pippy's influence – compliant, good girl, abides by the rules – and the other half of me is my French mother's side – 'Whoo-hoo! Let's go mad!'

I'm a bit like Maria in *The Sound of Music*: a sort of compliant nun with a really naughty side. I like it. It's enriching, and I wouldn't want to be all one or all the other. When my kids really need me to pull some serious mummy shit out the bag, I can totally do that. When they want me to go to a gig or act like a numpty, I can totally do that too. Anybody who's read an interview that I've done will know that I often drop myself right in it because my naughty, wanting-to-shock side will come out and I'll say something that turns into 'Pantgate' or 'Menopausegate'. I'm always a gnat's nose (that's really small) away from flashing my boobs on the red carpet. Everybody thinks I'm joking when I say that. I'm not. One day I would *love* to do it. When I'm sixty-five . . . Amazing. When Britney Spears shaved her head and everybody was going, 'Oh my God, she's completely lost it,' I so got it. I understand where it came from.

I'm really lucky that my wild child is kept in check (most of the time) by my compliant child, whereas my mum just had 100 per cent wild child and it was devastating for her. Later on in her life I hear she was a good stepmum, which I'm really pleased about, but to me and Caroline and to our family in France and to all of her boyfriends and previous husbands she was devastating in so many ways.

My mum moved around a lot, depending on who she was dating or married to, but her parents lived in the 8th arrondissement in Paris, which is right by the Champs-Élysées, and I would always stay with them when I was in Paris during school holidays. Their apartment was absolutely how you might imagine a posh French apartment to be, although it was very cheap as the rent was controlled and they'd been there for forty years. It had three bedrooms, a dining room, a living room, a TV/snug and a very tiny kitchen. My grandparents were called Olga and Pierre Hennion and they lived with their Portuguese maid, Maria, who was basically like a mother to my sister and, when I was there, to me too. My grandparents had their own bedrooms, and so whenever my mum split with a boyfriend she would come back and share Caroline's bedroom. She acted more like a sister than a mum, and it was Maria who told us to tidy up, not to come in too late, who vetted boy-friends . . . Caroline and I felt safe with Maria around.

My French grandparents were loving people but quite elderly and strict, probably a bit beyond wanting to bring up any more children. I think part of my mother's problem was that she needed somebody to invest time and effort into her, but I'm not sure her parents knew how to do that, so she went careering off the rails and nobody knew how to bring her back.

My mother would walk into a room, often a bit drunk, and I would look at her and think, 'Right, how am I going to play this? Should I be the sweet little daughter who's so happy to see her mother, cover her in kisses and sit on her lap, or should I be very, very quiet because she's annoyed and she's going to throw a tantrum, or should I play the cheeky chappie to coax her out of her bad mood?' She was so unpredictable that even when I did amazing things, she wasn't always pleased. When I passed my O Levels I called mum to tell her, but she was drunk. She said, 'Do you think I'm proud? Do you think I care? You're showing off. You're not the only one who's clever in this family.'

She was having a bad day and she didn't mean it, I know that now, but at the time it broke my heart. She was probably jealous of the opportunities I had because, by that age, she'd already had a baby.

As time went on I adapted myself more and more to make her happy, but I was losing more and more of myself. When I got clean, I tried to help her. I'd known for a long time that my mum was an alcoholic. After a particularly bad holiday with her, I wrote to her saying that I knew she had a drink problem because I had one too, and gave her the telephone numbers for a 12-step fellowship programme in South Africa, as she was about to move there. 'Please get clean. I can't see you like this any more, it's too painful.' She called me, very angry, shouting at me, and after we hung up I didn't speak to her for a few years. After she moved to South Africa she did actually get sober and we got back in touch.

Before I married Matthew, I contacted her. I was very excited about inviting her to our wedding. I wanted it to be an enormous building-of-bridges. She came to England, Matthew's family came over from America, and we all went out and had a great time.

A few nights before the wedding, she and I went to an NA meeting together and I held her hand through the whole thing. I'd always longed for a mum to hold hands with. A mum to go shopping with. A mum who, if I went into her bedroom after a nightmare, would lift up the duvet and pat the bed and say, 'Come and get into bed with me. Are you okay?' A mum who would notice if I was sad. A mum would who wipe the snot from my nose when I had a cold and hold my ponytail when I was throwing up. A mum who would notice if I'd gone missing or if I needed something. Those were the things that I yearned for; so sitting at this meeting with my mum who was not drinking and was there for me, for the first time ever, made me cry. It was an intense, beautiful moment that I will cherish for ever, despite what happened afterwards.

Matthew and I got married, it was a wonderful day, and then we went on honeymoon to a very glamorous island; but we got a bit bored so we cut it short by a week and went to Paris where we met up with my mum again. We had dinner together, and Matthew noticed something. She was telling stories about my childhood, but she was telling them from her perspective, as if they were funny. When *I* had told them to Matthew, they were sad. Matthew and I talked later about how my mum had no idea of the impact her behaviour had on anyone.

A few months after our wedding, Matthew took me to a lovely little hotel in Scotland as a treat for my birthday. In the morning, he came into our room looking really worried. He'd been downstairs to get the papers and he handed one to me. On the cover it said 'MUMMY, I NEED A MEETING.' My mum had sold a story about the time we'd gone to a meeting together. I'd been in NA for a long time, and my anonymity had never been blown, nobody had ever said anything, but there, in spectacular fashion, my own mother had blown my anonymity, and her own, on the front page of the *Daily Mirror*. It's the worst thing she could have done to me. You should never blow a person's anonymity because it can lead to relapse and relapse can lead to death.

She had even sold pictures of our honeymoon in Paris. I was very particular about not selling our wedding or our honeymoon – not that I judge anybody who does that, I'm always rather pleased when people do because I get to see lovely dresses in *Hello!* or *OK!*, but I just didn't want extra pressure on the day.

'Oh, I didn't think you'd mind,' she said when I called her. She really didn't see how it could have upset me. She had recently offered to fly my sister from England to South Africa and I'd wondered at the time how she could afford it. Once the article came out, I knew. It was the worst betrayal and she just didn't get it. I think she felt that she was celebrating me, but the article intimated that I was on the verge of relapsing before the wedding, that I'd gone to this meeting because I was in a bit of trouble. Actually, what the papers didn't put was that I was going to two or three meetings a week because I loved them and I was the happiest I'd ever been. I don't think I've been so hurt by anything in my whole life or so disappointed. I felt like I had been hit by a freight train. My sister, who hadn't once been mentioned by my mum in the article, as if she didn't exist, cancelled her trip to South Africa and never spoke to my mother again.

I *kept trying* to build bridges, I never stopped hoping something would change, but there were always disappointments. I gave her money every month to pay all her medical bills, she was poorly but clean, and she sent me an amazing four-page letter that I hoped would be the start of a new closeness. Matthew warned me not to hope and, sure enough, not long after she just asked for more and more money.

When she was really poorly, towards the end, I got a message from her about a journalist harassing her. She was asking me to get him off her back but when I contacted him, he told me that my mother's first question to him had been about how much she would be paid if she did an interview. I tried to talk to her but she'd gone AWOL, and when a big article came out in the *Daily Mail* I was surprised that it was not attacking me but her, because she had promised an interview, only given half of it, then disappeared. The journalist got the hump and wrote about what a flake she was and that he wasn't surprised I wouldn't see her. That didn't make me happy, it made me really sad, because I didn't want anybody to come out badly.

Then she got sicker and I kept wondering whether I should go over. At the time, I was trying to come to terms with why I was constantly striving to get my mother to be a mother when she clearly wasn't capable of doing that. I was still crying with this ache I had in my heart for somebody to mother me . . . not *anybody*, I wanted *my mother* to mother me. My granny's amazing, my stepmum is amazing, but I just wanted my mother to *want* to mother me and I didn't know how to come to terms with the fact that I could not make that happen.

A lot of people were telling me to go out and see her. I asked myself over and over, how will I feel if she dies? Will I be full of regret that I didn't take the children over to meet her? Will I feel okay with myself? Will I feel I've done right by her?

I know that I really tried to build bridges with my mother but it didn't work. My decision not to see her was to safeguard my own mental well-being. If I had felt there was any way that my children could safely meet their grandmother without her selling the story or photographs of them to the papers, I would have made it happen. But I just couldn't trust her.

That was a really big lesson for me. Whenever I'm in a situation I always think to myself, 'How am I going to feel at the end of this? Am I going to have any lasting regrets?' Even though a lot of people were telling me I would regret not seeing my mother again before she died, I *knew* in my heart I wouldn't and ... I haven't. For some people that is quite shocking because the mother–child bond is sacrosanct, it's the most precious thing in the whole world. I agree; but to my mind a parent's job is to safeguard their child, to nurture them and look after them. That's why I wanted to be a parent. Being a parent is to put your children above *you* and to put yourself out for them. My mother couldn't do that. That isn't how my mother–daughter relationship panned out, and all the chaos, the rejection and the selfishness damaged Caroline and me, and so we were estranged from our mum. But I'm okay with that and I am still okay with that now that mum's gone.

The experience of not visiting my mum before she died taught me a very crucial lesson.

If I make a decision that shocks others but is necessary for me, that's OK.

Jealousy

I used to be very jealous because I was super possessive of the people I loved. I was frightened somebody would take them away because I had such a fear of abandonment.

I can remember the first time I felt really jealous. I suppose I was about eight or nine and I had a friend over and my dad was down for the weekend and he started playing with her. She was really fun and they were laughing and I felt sick. I really, really hated her at that moment. She was a good friend but I still had these dark thoughts: 'Don't play with my dad, I never see him. I can't bear the fact that you are having a good time with him because *I* want to have a good time with him and you're taking him away from me.' I don't think I had another friend over at the weekend for a long time after that. I wanted to have my dad to myself.

This fear stayed with me later in life. I didn't like it if girls were coming on to my boyfriends. I've never had uncontrollable jealousy but I do remember, before I met Matthew, I was with various boyfriends (although Matthew likes to think he's the only one) who were naughty boys and I didn't feel completely secure with them; I think jealousy comes from insecurity. When you feel very secure and happy in yourself you don't really get jealous because there's nothing to be frightened of. Jealousy is an emotional reaction to an emotional situation and it's not the same as envy. Envy is when you are jealous of somebody's situation, the money or the opportunities that they have. Jealousy, for me anyway, was more to do with a fear of abandonment.

The way that I dealt with it when I was younger was to repeat a mantra in my head. 'The more jealous I get, the more I'm perpetuating the situation that will make me jealous. So if I get jealous with a boyfriend and say something stupid and jealous to him, he gets annoyed with me which makes the other girl who's not possessive with him seem much more interesting and funny so they'll probably talk more which makes me more jealous.' I know that's a long mantra! But it highlighted the futility of jealousy and how it just pushes the people you love further AWAY!

So, if you are feeling jealous, don't tell anyone, because it's really toxic and the only person it makes look bad is you. And if you are with somebody that you can't trust, *dump them*. If somebody you're with says, 'Oh God, you're so needy,' take note. You're only needy when your emotional needs are not being met. Dump them too!

Doing bad things does not mean you are a bad person

Generally I have been a very good girl, but sometimes good girls have to do something really naughty to break out. Which means I've done some really bad things, but that doesn't make me a bad person. I think, at times, I was possessed by a naughty imp, like the time I pushed Catherine Smith in the pool. Her surname wasn't actually Smith, but I don't want to blow her privacy.

Catherine was at my school and Pippy had invited her round to play. It was winter and we still lived in my granny and grandpa's big house with the pool and the old metal climbing frame beside it. We went outside to play but it was one of those play-dates when you get a bit bored, and you're not quite sure how to entertain yourselves.

Catherine was in her winter uniform and leaned right over the deep end of the pool, asking how deep it was. Then she crouched down, put her hand in the water and said, 'Ooh, it's cold.' I honest to God don't know what happened to me because without even thinking, with one solitary index finger, I gave her the gentlest little push. She just plopped in with a little roly-poly *plop*!

OMG, it was immediate horror! What had I done?! She was flailing around in the freezing water, and I grabbed her hands and pulled her out. I could see that she was winding up to a proper tantrum, which would have been my reaction too.

'Catherine, I'm so sorry! Please, please will you run round the garden? Please can you just run round the garden and get dry? Please don't tell my granny,' I kept saying.

Pippy came out and I'll never forget the look on her face. She was incredulous, horrified, like I was the spawn of Satan. Now that I'm a parent, I know she would have been wondering how the hell she was going to tell the girl's mother.

'What on earth possessed you?' she said. I'd never seen her like that. She was shaking and red.

'You, go upstairs to your bedroom and shut the door. You get bread and milk for dinner. Go ... NOW!' she whispered, furiously.

I don't know why I did it but I think I scared the bejesus out of Catherine. There's a strong chance she has forgotten about it but there's also a strong chance that it's ruined her entire life and every time she sees me on telly she wants to kill me. But what I'm trying to say to any parents out there is this: I was not a bad person, but I did do something that was really bad. Don't write a child off because they do one bad thing or make one heinous mistake (or, in my case, several).

Keep avenues of communication open

I'm a big believer in not carrying secrets and problems alone, but sharing them and lightening the load. I also think I should be as straightforward and honest with my kids as possible. No one told me that my mum was gone for good and I was going to be living with Pippy from then on. I don't blame anyone for that, it was how things were done, but maybe it would have helped me accept the situation rather than leaving me wondering what was happening. I felt like I couldn't ask about it.

Open communication is something that's really impor-tant to me. No problem is unsolvable and we can sort anything out together as a family. If any of my kids are having a hard time, and all of them have at some point, we all rally because it's a team effort and I want that child to know they are not alone.

Whatever my child told me, even if it was the most shocking thing that I had ever heard, I would do everything in my power not to show them that I was horrified. I would just say, 'Oh, right. Well, okay. How do you feel about that? What do you think? What do you want to do? How can I help you with that?' rather than going, 'Oh my God! I'm gonna phone their parents right now!' If I react like that, they're never going to tell me anything again because they don't want the drama. They just need help. I haven't experienced this yet, but I'm sure I will.

I'm a big believer in anything that creates the feeling that we're all in it together. I know as a recovering addict that isolation is dangerous. There's a great saying, 'An addict alone is in bad company.' You get stuck in your own thoughts and go to dark places. Seeking comfort with other people, knowing that you're not alone, is really important.

Pippy taught me a lot about this when I was eleven. She could tell that I really, really didn't want to go to school on Mondays but didn't want to talk about why. I was having a problem with one of my classes and didn't know how to share my eleven-year-old worries. One day Pippy left a book open with a pen, right next to where I was doing my homework. So I wrote down the problem I was just too embarrassed and anxious to talk about and closed the book. Pippy didn't do the big drama. She just went to my school and sorted it. I didn't want to worry my granny by telling her what was upsetting me, but her leaving the book open for me solved the problem (clever Pippy).

Matthew and I have very open communication with our kids but writing about that memory reminds me that I must put a book in their rooms so that they can write in it if ever they want to tell me something and they're too embarrassed to ask, the idea being 'Ask me anything, tell me anything. If you've written it in the book, I'll reply in the book.'

'I love you'

There's one book I vividly remember from when I was a kid. It's Paul Gallico's *The Day the Guinea-Pig Talked*. It's about a guinea pig and the little girl who owns him, and by magic they are given one minute to talk to each other. They are so overwhelmed by how much they want to say in that sixty seconds that they are speechless. I remember being *so* tense that they'll miss the opportunity to talk to each other, but just before time runs out they both say, 'I love you.'

I remember crying and crying at the ending. I suppose it was something to do with wanting to love or be loved in the way the little girl and the guinea pig loved each other. The little girl and the guinea pig had been thinking of all the things they wanted to say to each other, but actually there was only one thing that they **needed** to let each other know. They remembered to say it right at the very end of the time that they had: 'I love you'.

It was a bit similar with Matthew's dad, who we called Pops. He had four sons he took care of and provided for brilliantly, and Matthew loved talking to his dad, but Pops was never really verbally demonstrative in that way. He never said 'I love you' to his boys. I think he felt he didn't need to ... that they knew.

At the very end of his life, when Matthew's dad knew he was going to die, he said 'I love you' for the first time to his sons. I thought it was so beautiful that Pops experienced an outpouring of love and wanted to actually say that to his boys. It reminded me of the Paul Gallico book: that you have all this time to think about what you're going to say, and such complicated feelings and emotions, but ultimately all that matters is love. At the end of his life, all Pops really wanted to do was just love everybody. I think that it's an overwhelming feeling, isn't it? If someone said to me, 'You've not got long left,' I'd just want to let everybody know how much they mean to me. I guess that's the thing that resonated with me with that book: when it comes down to it, all you want to do is let the people you care about know that you love them. That's all that matters.

*

The healing power of music

Pippy taught me the importance of music and its healing properties and perhaps that's why I've been obsessed with music all my life. Music has helped me through some of the darkest times of my life and also carried me through some of the happiest. It is the only mood-altering drug I'm allowed, so I feast on it regularly.

There was always music playing in our house and there was a piano that I was encouraged to play. I remember when Pippy was really sad she wouldn't just cry, she would sing and cry. If there'd been an argument over lunch, when she was doing the washing-up afterwards she would belt out something like 'Don't Cry for Me Argentina' while crying. I always thought there was some sort of magical pathos in that. I would look at her in her rubber gloves at the sink, singing and crying. It was amazing.

I remember, when I was about fourteen, splitting up with a boy I'd kissed. I was convinced he was my boyfriend but I don't think he thought that at all. Suddenly he was with someone else and I was gutted. I remember listening to 'It's Over' by ELO again and again, singing and crying, just how Pippy taught me. The lyrics spoke to me. They were exactly how I was feeling. There's a magic that only really happens when you're getting into music in a big way, probably around thirteen, when lyrics become the soundtrack to your life until you're maybe twenty-two, twenty-three, when life's burdens start weighing you down and you never get the opportunity or the time to sit down and really engross yourself in lyrics again.

Music provokes feelings in a way that nothing else can. It can take me straight to a moment. So when Prince died, I put on his music and just cried, because he was the soundtrack to my twenties. His album *Sign o' the Times* is one of the most unbelievably brilliantly crafted pieces of music I think I've ever heard. Prince just didn't write conventionally. Not verse, chorus, verse, chorus, middle 8, key change, chorus, end. No . . . he told stories, mostly of pent-up sexual tension. His songs always end in what feels like an earth-shattering musical orgasm with a post-coital cigarette. David Bowie I played every time I got stoned. His music, like Prince's, you can never tire of because you hear something different every time you play it. *Enigma* makes me sob.

Today, for example, I'm not feeling very well. I've got a cold and a cough and I'm pretty pissed off about it. I was in the car earlier and I put on a song by a thrash metal band called Helmet. They did a collaboration with House of Pain. It's a great track and I listen to it when I'm fed up and I sing along at the top of my voice and let it all out. Or I might listen to Sepultura, a Brazilian thrash metal band, or Metallica. Oh my God, I love Metallica. I have a track for literally every single mood. I listen to glam rock, I love Calvin Harris, I love David Lee Roth, I love Rihanna, I love Beyoncé, Katy Perry, house music, country, I love old school, new school. The best songs of all are the ones that remind me of the children. Holly, Justin Bieber; Tilly, 'Stronger' by Clean Bandit, and Chester's is 'G6' by Far East Movement.

I remember my birthday the year the hurricane hit the UK. It was the night of the 15 October 1987, and my birthday is the 16th. I got up in the morning, put on my Walkman (remember those?!) and left the house. It was still really windy, no buses were running, and I walked from Hammersmith to Chelsea to get to work. As I was walking I was looking at everybody standing outside their houses with trees that had smashed through their roofs or crushed their cars and, bizarrely, I was listening to 'September' by Earth, Wind & Fire. It was really surreal, listening to such uplifting music with all the crazy carnage everywhere.

You've heard of a man cave? My man cave, or she shed, would be a mini nightclub where I could crack out my amazing vinyl and play incredibly loud music without disturbing anybody else.

The Ultimate Playlist in My She Shed

'Stronger' by Clean Bandit

'I Found Lovin'' by Fatback Band

'Feel So Real' by Steve Arrington

'Icarus' by Madeon

'Real Joy' by Fono

'Cool' by Alesso

'212' by Azealia Banks

'Biz Is Goin' Off' by Biz Markie

'Three Little Words' by Frankmusik

'Too Good' by Drake

We can learn from each generation

For most of my childhood my great-grandmother, Mickey's mother, lived with us and, of course, I was living with my granny and my auntie. It was Pippy who really showed me how much older people have to offer; in the McCall family, the elderly are revered. We learn so much from each generation of our family and there is a wonderful sense of security in keeping generations together. We had a sort of Mediterranean thing going on. In Italy, Spain and France, elders are respected.

In our family, the older you are, the wiser you are.

You don't become less valuable or less relevant, you become more relevant, more valuable, more *interesting*. My granny and great-granny have been a huge source of knowledge and security for me, and it is really precious and very important to me that my children are learning that lesson too, in the same way I did. I have recreated what I had as a child. Pippy lives close to us and my kids see their great-granny just like I did.

I have lovely memories of sitting at my great-granny's feet and pinching the skin on the back of her hand and watching how slowly it would go down. She was really good about it because I was probably quite annoying. I mean, it's probably pretty depressing having a littler person play with your saggy skin, but she let me do it all day long and I'd stroke the lovely soft tops of her arms – what we'd now call 'bingo wings', but I loved her bingo wings and she let me just sort of squish them like a cuddly toy. She'd save me the crust of her stoneground bread and I'd put butter on it and watch TV with her after school.

I know not everybody can have their grandparents living with them, it's a question of space, so I'm in a really lucky position, because having Pippy in our lives enriches it. I think because we appreciate her she is always happy to see us. She never says, 'You don't see me enough. Why don't you visit more?' She's just a really positive person.

If I'm in a tiswas I go and sit at Pippy's feet and put my head in her lap and she strokes my head. She knows how to make me feel better, and when she does that I think she feels better too. I need her and she needs me. It's nice. She's got dementia, so she can't necessarily always remember my name, but she knows me and I still get that feeling, that amazing feeling, of comfort from her. I can just sit with my head in her lap and she'll give me these golden nuggets of advice.

In my family we have an expression, 'Pippy knows'; because my granny has given me loads of amazing advice over the years and still does. By the time I hit my teenage years and moved to London to live with my dad and stepmum, Pippy had crammed me full of really good, in some ways quite old-fashioned, values and morals and beliefs and for that I am eternally grateful, because when I did go careering off the rails I think the reason I didn't entirely sink was because at the very heart of me, in my core, is a really strong set of values and I owe that all to my granny.

*

What 'Pippy knows':

1. Whatever life throws at us, we will just get up, dust ourselves off, get back on the horse and get going again.

2. There is great value in routine and the stability that a routine can bring. There are rituals that I do in my family today that I did as a child with Pippy. One day a week was sweetie day, and Pippy would give me 10p to go to the sweetie shop. In our house, Sunday is sweetie day, and we do that religiously. The kids are allowed to go down and choose three tiny sweets on a Sunday and we try to avoid them the rest of the week.

3. Be brave in the face of pain. Pippy was nigh on impossible to give sympathy to. Really horrific things would happen to her and she was always so brave about it. 'Pippy's fine! Everything's fine!' she would say. She severed quite a few toes from one foot by running them over with a rotary mower. I found her on the phone to the ambulance with a very bloody tea towel wrapped round her foot.

   'Pippy, are you okay?' I must have been about seven or eight.

   'Pippy's fine! Everything's okay.' I look back now and think, 'God, she was strong.'

4. Never complain. I don't remember Pippy ever complaining, even when my grandparents had a big change in circumstances and had to move out of the house that I know she loved very, very much. It was the perfect family home. I

think they'd been there for fifteen or twenty years and it had really been the McCall stronghold. Due to a change in finances they had to move to a small cottage and I know that was very difficult for Pippy, but you would never have known it. She made the new place into a fantastic home and never complained.

5. Pippy taught me the value of family.

6. She taught me how to speak my mind.

7. Pippy taught me that a woman can do any job a man can do. She was always doing jobs around the house that are usually considered a 'man's' job. She was a strong, independent woman and taught me how to be one too.

8. Be kind. Pippy lived on her own just outside of Guildford for many years after Mickey died. She was always busy. She would visit people in the old people's home up the road, invite the vicar round, help at the church, arrange the flowers, go to watercolour painting classes. She was busy, busy, busy, always giving, always doing something for other people, and as she got older, she reaped the rewards for being a genuinely brilliant human being. When she needed something or when she was struggling, people rallied around and supported her. There's a lovely couple who come and visit her now, the husband was the son of Pippy's best friend from school who she really helped when his mum was very poorly. He's now in his sixties, but he's never forgotten Pippy for that. She has just been a good

person and when you're a good person it comes back to you.

9. Get involved. Pippy taught my dad, and my dad taught me, that we always get involved, we never cross the road. If I see somebody in trouble or something bad's happening, I don't think twice about getting in there and trying to stop it. That might not be the safest option and I know I'd fret if my kids started doing it, but that's just who we are. Pippy's always been a very political person as well and I really respect that. She's taught us all to stand up, make ourselves heard and that our votes count.

10. It was Pippy who taught me about charity. When I was a kid she helped raise funds for a charity called Action Research for the Crippled Child, now known as Action Medical Research – they discovered the polio vaccine way back when, and more recently devised cooling therapy and the Nuchal scan, and they're doing lots of research into Duchenne muscular dystrophy and other rare childhood diseases. I still do maybe three or four events for them a year to raise money, and lots of other events for charity. It's a win–win thing – charity helps other people, but it also makes you feel good.

11. Pippy taught me that our elders can be a massive inspiration. Pippy lost her father at quite a young age to alcoholism. I think the First World War was very, very tough on a lot of men, and he was in a bad way. After he

died, Lulu, Pippy's mum, despite having five children, started a catering business that was hugely successful. For a widow, a mother of five, in the thirties, post-war, to start a business and be totally kick-arse and make an absolute fortune – enough of a fortune to employ nannies and buy a really nice house – is just amazing. I remember being quite frightened of her! She was a strong, no nonsense woman. The McCall women, we're no pushovers!

Surviving school

I suppose I must have started at my primary school about a year after my mum left me with Pippy. I made lots of friends and most of the time I was very happy living with Pippy and having my dad and then my dad and Gaby coming down at weekends.

I was six when Dad married Gaby (I was a bridesmaid at their wedding), and quite soon afterwards they broached the subject to my grandparents of me coming to live with them in London, and actually, if somebody had said to me, 'Would you like to go and live with your dad and stepmum?' I'd have just said yes immediately. But they didn't so I didn't. It was quite stressful for my dad and my stepmum, spending all those years coming down every weekend when they would have dearly loved me to live with them, but Pippy, who is extremely forceful, always argued, 'Wouldn't it be better to leave it till eleven? She needs to finish primary school. It's just four more years . . . blah, blah, blah.' So I stayed and stayed and stayed. No hardship . . . just a fact.

After a while I began to feel a bit different to the other kids. I suppose, in part, it was because I was the only kid who lived with their grandparents and not their parents. Then when I was nine my granddad lost all his money in a bad investment, and by the time I was eleven I started to feel a bit penalised at school for not having money when everybody around me did. We'd moved to the cottage and Pippy drove an old Renault 4 when everybody else had a BMW. Very sadly, stupid things like not having a watch or not going on foreign holidays started to bother me. Looking back I can see that my life was great. My dad and my stepmum made it clear that they really loved me and I'd often go away with them somewhere at the weekend. They had lots of friends around the country so they'd come and pick me up and we'd drive to Cornwall or to Wales and we'd all go on big family holidays to Devon together or we'd go and see my stepmum's mum in Sussex. I had everything I needed, but I ended up feeling that somehow it wasn't enough to fit in at school.

Also, I suppose, it was hard having this double life that I couldn't talk about. I learned quite quickly not to be 'different', not to talk about my life in France at school, or at home. There was often really crazy stuff going on with my mum and in my French family, but I couldn't talk to Pippy even about the things that were only slightly bothering me, let alone the worst stuff, in case she stopped me going. I loved my sister and I loved my French grandparents and I loved my mum (you might not understand that, but I did) and I didn't want anybody to stop me going. So I knew that all this crazy, crazy stuff was going down but I couldn't tell anybody at home because I was frightened that they wouldn't let me go back, and I couldn't really share with anyone at school because I just wanted to be like everyone else. That was a weird one, because I probably did need to talk it through a little bit with someone ... ANYONE!

My sister was really the only other person who really knew what was going on with my mum, but I was six years younger than her, so I was really quite annoying. By the time I got to fourteen and she was twenty we started getting much closer. By then she'd gone through her wild-child phase and was staying in more, not going clubbing so much, trying to be a mother to me. Once I was in my teens, she used to look after me when I was in Paris. She'd say, 'You've got to be in by this hour. Make sure you come in before Granny wakes up. Be safe, make sure you stay with so-and-so – they'll look after you.' She was such a calming figure for me, and an amazing hugger.

My mum, on the other hand, saw me as a mascot. I remember going on holiday with her to Île de Ré one summer, when I was twelve. She took me and my sister out clubbing, which I suppose was better than cancelling the holiday at the last minute because she didn't have childcare for me, and I remember being in this nightclub, wearing a lovely knee-length pink dress with lace gloves and ankle boots and my hair up with a big bow in it. I was hanging out near the DJ, chatting to him, and I remember at one point sitting on his lap and saying, 'Guess how old I am.' I mean, disaster waiting to happen . . .!

Seventeen?'

'No . . .'

My mum had left the club to buy some weed and she'd been gone so long I was sure she'd forgotten about me, so I was relieved to have the DJ to talk to.

'Sixteen?'

'No.'

She'd been smoking 'magic cigarettes' all my life and from about eight years old I knew what they were. I couldn't see Caroline. She was somewhere in the club, talking to some boys.

'OK, fifteen?'

'No . . . thirteen!'

I remember being really pleased that the DJ thought I was so old, but when I told him my real age he had this expression on his face that said, 'Okay, that's seriously not good,' and he immediately stopped talking to me. So I wandered off, looking for my mum, and began getting unwanted attention from some boys trying to put their arms around me and stuff. I always gave off this air of 'I'm fine, I'm cool, I know what I'm doing', but suddenly I didn't know what I was doing and was really scared.

'I don't feel safe,' I thought, panicky, looking around for my mum, but she was nowhere to be found. It was Caroline, my protective big sis, who waded in and got rid of those boys for me.

Obviously, I couldn't tell anyone in England about what

went on or they'd stop me going, so I suppose that also made me feel very different to my friends at school.

My first year of secondary school was tough. I was unhappy and people were not that nice to me. By then, I really, really wanted to be with my dad and my stepmum. That feeling was getting more and more intense so, eventually, my stepmum and my dad had a conversation with me about it and I said, 'Yes, I really want to come and live with you.'

'Okay, well, we're going to have to present a united front to Pippy.'

Pippy was heartbroken. It was like losing a child for her. I was thirteen by then, a teenager, and I just wanted to be in London with my parents. Leaving Pippy was really sad and very difficult for us all, but Pippy's amazing and she's all about 'forgive and forget'. So I left that school and moved out of Pippy's house and went to live with my dad and my stepmum in London and carried on going to Paris to visit my mum, my sister and my French grandparents.

Quite soon after I moved to London, Gaby had a baby. They had been trying for eight years to get pregnant and then I moved in with them and a few months later she was pregnant. My stepmum always said that she thought that it was because I'd gone to live with them and they no longer had the stress of going down to see me every weekend and me crying every Sunday night. That made me feel special.

On my first day at the new school in London, I turned up with a pudding-bowl haircut, my uniform socks pulled up to my knees, my A-line skirt down to the knee with a WHSmith doctor's bag and pristine uniform. It was very obvious that I was fresh from the country.

I stood in the doorway looking around and thought, 'I'm gonna die.' I saw skinheads and girls with pink hair. No one was wearing uniform socks, everybody had pink or green socks and they were all ankle socks, and everybody had the same green canvas bag from Millets with the names of bands I'd never heard of written on them. I thought, 'This is not going well. This is a bad first day.'

A girl called Katie walked up to me and said, 'Hi. Come in. Are you new?' At that moment I made the decision to change myself. Adapt and survive. Within two days I had cut my hair, peroxided it blonde, no more knee-high socks. I took my skirt in and up, binned the WH Smith bag and got the Millets canvas bag and wrote the names of lots of bands that I'd never heard of on it. Katie let me into her gang, there were about seven of us and we were thick as thieves. We wore the same clothes in and out of school, constantly slept over at each other's houses; Katie's parents took us in all the time. She and I are still great mates, I'm godmother to her daughter. They were good times.

That experience taught me about adapting to my environment. I'm not saying that's always the right thing to do – I love people who stand out from the crowd – but I think at school it was a necessity for me to survive. At school, all anybody wants to do is fit in. I didn't want to be different from everybody else. I didn't want to look different. When I moved to London, feeling different just disappeared. I was with my dad and my stepmum, we lived really close to the school and our house was normal for the area. Everything about me suddenly became normal. It felt really great. I could just blend in.

My kids are the same, which is why, as a parent, when I do the school run I don't wear my favourite, bright green fake-fur calf-length coat in which I resemble a lawn, because the kids want me to look like everybody else's mother, not a TV personality but a mummy. They don't want me shouting hello or being over the top, they just want me to be normal. (I save the OTT stuff for the weekends!)

The minute I left school, or in sixth form really, I started discovering my individuality, but what I loved about the London school was that money was not a thing. I'd come from somewhere where money was a thing and it made me feel quite isolated to have had money and then lost it and to be made to feel less for not having it. It made me really value the idea of friendship regardless of what you've got. Who you are is more important than what you've got.

If, unlike me, you don't, can't or won't blend in, BRAVO! If you're really confident it doesn't matter what you look like or where you're going or who you are. The minute you let people chink away at that confidence, it's like a crack in a rock when water gets in and turns into ice. It expands and chips away another bit of rock so more water can get in. Be confident . . . *Vive la différence!*

I think the best way to armour my kids with confidence is to give them the gift of humour. Matthew's amazing at this. He won't mind me saying that he had a rotten time at school

– he is dyslexic and was told he was stupid the whole time when he's super bright. So when people say something bad to Matthew or embarrass him, he laughs his way out of it and that's been an amazing tool for our kids. 'How can I make this situation funny?'

Funny is disarming.

People don't really know what to do with funny. They want you to hurt. So we started quite young showing our kids how to contradict and meet cruelty with humour. Even when ours were six, seven or eight, when someone upset them by sticking their tongue out, we taught them not to turn away and be sad, because that's what the bullies want. We suggested a big smile and a thumbs-up, a 'Thanks!' and a laugh. It worked.

Change your hair!

If there's anything really intense happening in your life and you're in emotional turmoil, don't hurt yourself, change your hair. It's a way of radically doing something to yourself that's noticeable, mood-altering, exciting and fun and your hair will always grow back. I have done this A LOT. This lesson is not sponsored by Garnier.

*

Never borrow your daughter's clothes

I remember, I must have been sixteen or seventeen, buying this amazing dress from Fiorucci, which at the time was *the* big brand. I look at old photos and I looked lovely, but I had this weird combo of quite a big ego and cripplingly low self-esteem. I had the confidence you get from being in the party scene, going out a lot, but inside I was thinking, 'Oh, I hate myself and my body, I'm so fat, look at my legs, oh, my bum's so big, oh, I look so ugly, this dress doesn't suit me, I look fat in everything.' I had this awful voice that was going on and on and on and on, and, thank God, I've stamped it out now, but at the time it was VERY LOUD, like most teenagers, I would imagine.

Anyway, I was so excited about this dress from Fiorucci. It was a bodycon dress and had a zip all the way down that you could seductively unzip a little bit to show some cleavage. It made me feel incredible and whenever I wore it people would go, 'Wow, you look amazing!'

One day, my mum asked if she could borrow my very special Fiorucci dress. I was a bit like, 'Oh, that's my favourite . . .' but I told myself not to be mean and selfish and said, 'Yeah, of course you can.' In truth, I really didn't want to lend it to her! She put it on and my heart really, really sank because she was asking again and again, 'Do I look all right? Do I look okay?' And all I could think was, 'Oh my God, she looks amazing,' and it was so, so, so, so depressing. My mum looked way hotter than me in my favourite dress, like WAY HOTTER.

At that moment I already knew what kind of a parent I was going to be, and I made a mental note:

I will never borrow my daughter's clothes for fear that
I might make her feel anything other than glorious
in her own skin.

In fact, my eldest daughter is always borrowing my clothes and looks *way* better than me in them, which is exactly how it should be! Way to go, Holly!

Do homework on Friday

I think a really good way to have a brilliant life is to do all the stuff you really don't want to do first. Get the yucky stuff out of the way and then you can have fun. We all are guilty of leaving the things we dread until last. I remember with home-work, I would have this nagging fear all through the weekend about Sunday night, because I would leave my homework until then. There'd be tears, it was awful. Then I read *The Road Less Travelled* by M. Scott Peck and he says to do the rubbish stuff first, then you can enjoy yourself. I wish I'd learned at school to do my homework on Friday and feel brilliant all weekend.

*

My dad is my hero

This isn't really a lesson, but my dad is so important to me he deserves a whole chapter to himself. A whole book. My dad is my hero.

My dad is the bravest man I know. He's got Alzheimer's. He's probably had it for about four or five years but we've only known what it is for a year and a half, and he's coping with such great dignity. It's tough on both him and Gaby, really tough, but he's not taking it lying down. He's such a fighter. Whenever I say to him, 'How's things?' he's always replies, 'I feel really good at the moment.' ♥ him. When he told my granny, his mother, who's also got vascular dementia, that he had Alzheimer's, it was so moving. She just cupped his head in her hands and told him he was very brave. He's always been my hero and he always will be.

I remember particularly when I was nineteen and my French grandfather died. He was called Pierre but was known as Pasha, and crikey, he was an intense man. A self-made millionaire who I thought did brilliantly, because he'd spent every centime of his fortune by the time he died; quite an achievement really. He spent it on himself and his family. He used to spoil me rotten when I went over there. We didn't have much money when I was living with Pippy and Mickey, we had a very different lifestyle in the UK compared to this slightly flamboyant, wild lifestyle that my sister and my French grandparents had in Paris.

My grandfather was enormous and smoked cigars all the time while my grandmother was tiny, Spanish-Algerian, brought up in France and unbelievably elegant in her high-waisted black capri pants with a fitted white shirt. She had short black hair and looked just extraordinary, in an Audrey Hepburn kind of way.

When my grandfather died I went to Paris to be with my sister Caroline and my French family for the funeral. When I arrived, I knew things were bad because my mum, upset and struggling, had gone on an absolute whopper bender. It was like some mad French farce – everyone grieving, everyone trolleyed. There was an awful moment when the undertakers couldn't get Pasha's coffin out of the door of their Paris flat. It was so undignified. They had to tip it up a little bit and we heard his body thud. Like I said . . . a mad French farce.

Nothing had been organised for the funeral, and my mum was drinking so that wasn't going to change. Normally I could help her through a bad patch but nothing I did was working, so I called my dad and begged him for help. He, heroically, got on the next plane. I told my mum that he was coming out and that he could help her organise the funeral and she seemed quite relieved and grateful. She drove me to pick him up from the airport but she was absolutely mullered. Since she wouldn't let me wear a seatbelt I was in the front seat, with my hands on the dash just thinking, 'Please, don't let me die.'

Suddenly she swerved off the road on a 'short cut', basically off-road through a forest, and we got grounded on a log. She got out of the car, it was dark and raining, I was crying because we were so late for my dad, and she flagged down some random car from the main road. The people in it were all looking at me like 'You poor sausage, she's quite clearly drunk and obviously you can't tell us how upset you are but we can see it in your face.' They helped us off the log and when we finally turned up at Charles de Gaulle Airport, very, very late, she mounted the pavement and said, 'Just run in and see if you can find him.'

Everything was closing down for the night – it was thirty years ago, airports weren't as busy in the evenings then. It must have been about 9 p.m. It's a circular airport so I was just running round and round screaming, 'Daddy? Daddy? Daddy?!' There were no mobile phones, no way of getting in touch with him; he could have been anywhere.

Then I saw him; six foot three with big, broad shoulders, carrying a briefcase and his overcoat and, oh my God, he just looked so sane and safe and strong. I ran into his arms. 'Oh my God, thank you, you're here. It's totally and utterly mad. Thank you, thank you, thank you.'

He did everything. He couldn't have been more perfect.

He was so nice. He was so understanding. He said to Mum, 'You must be so upset and tired. Why don't I drive?' not, 'Crikey, you've been drinking,' which would have made her savage. That night was really weird because I'd never been on my own with my mum and dad that I could remember. It felt so strange, I didn't really like it, my two worlds colliding.

Me and Dad slept on a sofabed while my mum walked around the kitchen, naked, clanging pans and making lots of noise. I think she was trying to flirt with him or be noticed in some way, but he'd been with my stepmother for thirteen years by then so it was not okay for her to behave like that. I was mortified, so embarrassed for Dad . . . and for myself.

During the funeral my poor mum was bereft, and plastered. There was a low mist and it was really eerie and silent when they opened the tomb to get the coffin in. Again, to our absolute horror, it didn't fit and they had to get a jackhammer out. A jackhammer! (#frenchfarce) If it hadn't been for my dad, I don't know how we'd ever have arranged the funeral at all.

It was my dad who showed me that being kind and giving and generous to people around you (I'm not talking about financially) makes you feel good too. He didn't have pots of money to give me, but he always had a paintbrush in his hand for every flat I moved into, and my stepmum was amazing like that too. OMG, she cried when she saw the first flat that I moved to when I left home, it was that bad, but they were right there, trying to make it homely! Their boot was always full of gubbins from moving me from place to place. They were always helping me cook when I had friends round, or they'd bring round some baking or pick something up for me. Always. It made me feel cherished and loved, and it made them feel good too.

So what I'm trying to tell you is that my dad is my hero and always has been. He was my 'Phone a Friend' when I did *Who Wants to Be a Millionaire?* He is so clever. Every now and again, I decide that I'm going to expand my brain and learn things. One of these times, I went into a bookshop and walked past the bestsellers and bought a book by Jonah Goldberg about how fascism has become a right-wing thing but was born out of communism. I thought it sounded incredibly educational and the cover had a smiley face on it. I was a child of the eighties, so smiley faces talk to me. So, I went on holiday to the South of France and started reading. Literally, at the end of every page, I'd call my dad and say, 'Dad, what does this mean?' Poor guy. He held my hand through the whole book. After that I thought, 'I've got to go back to Marian Keyes . . . I can't do this.' I love Marian Keyes. On top of being handsome and clever (BTW, in case you don't love my dad enough already) HE'S A NEW MAN. He cooks, irons and cleans. I know!!

My dad is everything.

I had a hero in my life. I was lucky. But even if I hadn't, I'd like to think I could be a hero for somebody else. It makes all the difference.

2

Lessons for Getting Back on Track

It's a true friend who's honest

I use the word 'hate' so rarely, it's such a strong word, but I really hated myself in my early twenties. I'd got to a stage where I just felt like I was good for nothing, a total waste of space. The drink and drugs were getting serious, not just a party thing any more, and I was a mess. Every morning I would wake up and say to myself, 'This is it, I'm not doing it again, I'm *definitely* not taking drugs today.' Then something would happen, bad or good.

'I'm just going to get some drugs to celebrate,' or 'I'm just going to get some drugs to commiserate,' I'd say, and be off again.

The most important thing was always hiding my habit so no one knew, and for years I would pride myself on the fact that no one could guess that I was off my face. I always felt like I was keeping it together while those around me were losing it. But this façade was getting harder and harder to maintain. The physical signs of drug addiction were beginning to show. There's a look that a junkie has that's a little bit shiny, a little bit grey, a little bit plasticky. I was a bit glazed and would occasionally just nod off (which is another sign), but I thought nobody could tell because my eyes are so dark brown you can't see if my pupils are big or small. Despite my habit, I was looking pretty good. I had bob-length brown hair and was in good shape from all the clubbing and dancing, so I fooled pretty much everyone. I had started meeting a few people who were recently clean from drink and drugs, but I'd look at them and think, 'You can't possibly be genuinely clean. Nobody's really clean.' I felt so powerless, like *I* just couldn't do it. Every time I tried and failed to get clean, I hated myself a little bit more. I felt like my life was a house of cards and that any minute I would bring the whole lot tumbling down on myself.

I had a boyfriend, who I'd been with on and off for six years. I lived with him and we were pretty serious, but we'd got into drugs together and were sliding down the slippery slope. By the time I was twenty-four and he was thirty, we'd both spent about a year and a half trying to stop. I was *extremely* manipulative, so whenever I failed to stop, I would somehow manipulate things to make it appear that it was *his* fault I'd started again. I was lying through my teeth to everyone, including him, about how many drugs I was taking.

Finally, I decided that to get clean, I needed a complete

change. I left my boyfriend and quit my job at Models 1. I admitted to some of the stuff I'd been doing to my dad and stepmum although the full debrief didn't happen until I'd committed to getting clean.

'I'm a mess, can I come home?' I said to them.

'Sure,' they said.

I assumed then, since it was 'my boyfriend's fault that I took drugs', I'd stop after we split. But no … I got worse. Without him holding me back, I got into a really bad way. For the first time, I became physically addicted to heroin. I wasn't injecting, I thought only horrible street junkies injected, but I was feeling the physical withdrawals if I didn't have it.

I was penniless. I had a beat-up old VW but not enough money to put petrol in it. I needed to get away … run away. I spoke to my mum and she said, 'Come and stay with me for a couple of weeks.' At that time she was living in Morocco, married to a guy who worked for the South African Embassy. Caroline and I decided we'd go there together, because I found my mum quite hard on my own, and I thought, 'This is a really good opportunity to wean myself off heroin. I've clearly got a heroin problem. I don't want to stop drinking, so I'm not going to go to AA, and I don't want to stop taking other drugs. I've just got a problem with heroin. So I'll carry on with alcohol and the other drugs and I'll be fine.'

I decided not to tell my mum anything about my habit. I was so ashamed. I would never admit to anybody that I'd taken heroin. The only people who knew also took it. I thought it was horrific that I was using, I disgusted myself, but I was convinced that I wasn't a 'junkie'. So I got some methadone, went to Morocco, and after two weeks I'd weaned myself off the gear and was feeling amazing.

Then a friend asked me to go to Florida with her. She was modelling for a shoot there and needed some help looking after her son. So I went out to Florida clean and feeling better than I had in years. Her baby was gorgeous and I had fun with them, got a tan, felt great and looked it.

When I returned to London I went back to running a Monday night – best night of the week – at this nightclub called Green Onions. Prince came one night, that was pretty cool. I went there and a friend of mine gave me some cash that he owed me from the nights he'd run while I was away. So I had a bit of cash in my hand and after three glasses of wine I was feeling a bit tipsy and somebody said, 'Do you want a line?'

'I shouldn't really, but it's just a line,' I thought. 'I'll just have one.'

So I had one line and about ten minutes later I bought half a gram. About an hour and a half later I bought another gram and then I went back to someone's house at the end of the night. At three o'clock in the morning I bought more coke from a dealer who was there. Everybody left. At eight or nine o'clock in the morning the guy whose flat it was said, 'I think you need to go because I have a flight to catch.'

'Oh no, no, no, no, I don't want to leave,' I said. I was so upset with myself I didn't want to be alone. I knew that when I left that flat it would really floor me that I had totally messed up that amazing, squeaky-clean person who had come back from Florida. For that month in Morocco and Florida I'd run away from the English Davina and turned into wonderful, healthy, fit Davina.

*I knew that when I left that flat I'd have to come to terms with the fact that I didn't just have a problem with heroin. I had a problem with **all** drugs, and far from me not being an alcoholic, I was a total alcoholic, because every time I had one drink it would take me straight to the drugs again.*

Suddenly it was as clear as flipping day. I felt really depressed. I was grieving for the fact that I would have to give everything up. I went back home and lay in bed feeling terrible. Then my best friend Sarah (Sozzlepots I call her) said, 'Do you want to come to a Santana concert tonight?'

'I'll see Sarah. She'll make me feel better,' I thought.

She came to pick me up and I got into the car with her. Then she said, 'Listen, I need to talk to you about something, because since you've been away everybody's been gossiping about you. You're the subject at every dinner party I go to and you are my best friend and you're a wreck. Unless you do something about it you're going to end up in serious trouble. You're letting everyone down and you're letting yourself down. I *know* you're lying to me and I know what you're doing. I *know* you've been taking heroin. You think that nobody else knows because you're trying to hide it, but everybody knows,' she said. It was like being hit by a freight train because I'd always felt I was above other drug addicts because I didn't steal, I had worked three jobs to get the money, I wasn't a street junkie, I didn't inject and, crucially, I was sure I had hidden my habit from everyone. It was like somebody had just put a dagger in my heart and twisted it hard. I was *so* convinced that I was not the same as any other junkie.

After a stunned silence I got so angry I called her every name under the sun. 'I'm fine! I'm fine! I've been away and I'm fine,' I was shouting as I got out of the car and slammed the door. I stormed back into my dad and stepmum's flat, where I was sleeping on a camp bed in a walk-in cupboard with a desk in it. I sat on the camp bed and cried and cried and cried and cried. I was furious with Sarah for a few hours and then I just . . . surrendered. I knew that everything she said was true.

'Oh my God, it's got to stop. I've got to stop,' I thought. 'I can't do this any more.'

I felt like I was on a merry-go-round. I could see life was happening off the merry-go-round. I could see it was happening and everybody was having a good time and I couldn't get off the merry-go-round. I couldn't make it stop.

The next morning I felt so rough I decided it was time to go to a Narcotics Anonymous meeting. I'd heard about them and knew a lovely girl called Mary who was in recovery. I was not looking forward to 'fessing up that I was not just casually taking drugs, and was convinced that when I called Mary she'd say, 'Oh my God, are you a user?!' But she just told me that there was a meeting at six o'clock and offered to meet me there.

When I put the phone down I thought, 'Oh my God, I've got an actual arrangement with somebody. Now I've got to go.'

Then I went to see Sarah, who I thought would never speak to me again after the language I'd used. On the way I stopped off and bought her a little bunch of flowers. I walked into her office and sheepishly apologised. I explained that I knew she was right ... that I was going to a meeting and I wanted it to change. Thank God, Sarah could see that I was different. There was a new humility in my voice, not the arrogance drugs gave it. She forgave me, and we both had a massive cry.

I went to the meeting that evening and my life changed. I thought everybody would hate and judge me but nobody did. In fact that girl on a camp bed, who had nothing to offer anyone, who wasn't famous, was asked out for coffee afterwards, and they bought it because I had not a pot to piss in. Somebody suggested that I go to ninety meetings in ninety days and I did a lot more than that. I was doing a couple a day most of the time. Things began to change and life began to change, all because a brave friend was honest.

I've done it a few times myself now, been very honest with a friend, and it's frightening. Two things happen. Firstly, it's a massive weight off your shoulders because carrying somebody else's deception, pretending you don't know, is really hard work. Secondly, that person might never come back to you. But Sarah showed me that night that being honest can save a person's life. She is the Cristina Yang to my Meredith Grey.

Thank you, Sarah; you are my person.

To be lovable, you have to love yourself

How did I stop completely hating myself? I took small steps. I sat at the front at meetings, I looked people in the eye, I learned to smile at strangers, I made literally thousands of cups of tea and I learned to communicate by saying, 'Do you want your coffee black or white or with sugar?' These were all quite big steps for me, to feel worthy of talking to other people. But the biggest lesson in self-acceptance came from Adela. She helped me in my early years of being clean and right at the beginning she could see this toxic self-loathing I was nurturing.

She gave me a mirror and told me to look in it every morning and night and say, 'I love you.'

I thought, 'Ugh, God, how hippy-dippy, how embarrassing!' She said, 'Just give it a try.' It felt so arrogant, to say 'I love you' to myself, but she pointed out that loving yourself doesn't mean that you think you're the best thing since sliced bread. It means that you love yourself even though you are not perfect, you love yourself warts and all. It means accepting that you are on a journey and there are bits of you that will improve and there are bits of you that you'll be working on for the rest of your life, but all of you is lovable. *To be lovable, you have to love yourself.*

'Oh God, when you put it like that . . .' I thought. So I put the mirror on my bedside table, face down, and it sat there for a month. I was in so much pain that I even avoided speaking to this friend because I couldn't tell her that I hadn't done it. She called and left messages and I felt so guilty that in the end I made myself pick up that mirror. I looked in it and just started crying. I put it straight back on the bedside table, face down, and laughed at myself, thinking, 'What is wrong with you?' So I called her and admitted that I hadn't been looking in the mirror for the past month, I'd been avoiding it, but that I'd just tried and burst into tears. What was wrong with me? She told me it was normal and to try 'I like you.'

So I went back to the mirror and every day I would have some strange reaction. Sometimes I'd pick it up and cry. Other times I'd be trying to say 'I like you' and would start laughing and put it down again. Finally, I managed to get out 'I like you' and then really, really, *really* cried.

'My God, it's taken me this long to come to terms with the person that I am enough to just say "I like you, you're okay,"' I thought. 'I've got to do that twice a day? This is arduous.'

After a while (it felt like a very long while) I could smile and say, 'I like you.' I began to believe that I was an okay person who generally tried to do the right thing and apologised when I failed. I came to understand that the feelings I'm left with if I don't do the right thing make saying 'I like you' quite difficult and so I try and live a life that enables me to look in the mirror and say 'I like you.'

Then I had to move on to 'I love you.' That felt like a big step. It took a year and lots and lots of work on myself before I could say it. I wrote a lot, to try and understand the things that were holding me back and blocking my happiness. Now I can quite easily say I love myself, although I always feel the need to explain that because I'm British. It's not arrogance, I don't think I'm perfect, but I know in my heart that I mean well, that I'm a good person, that I try my best at everything. So the lesson I've learned from my long, long journey to self-love, is that it's absolutely worth the effort.

Forgive and accept yourself

Forgiving and accepting yourself is crucial to self-love.

By 'forgiving yourself' I mean forgiving yourself for all the things you don't like about yourself and anything you might have done in the past that you are not proud of. Believe me when I say I had a long list of things I wasn't proud of. You *can* start again and feel better. Feeling guilty about the past just makes us less likely to do better in the future. Whether or not other people find it in their hearts to forgive us is their problem.

I need a lot less self-forgiving when I feel self-accepting, because I don't get myself into the messes that I did in the past. Self-acceptance means learning to like myself as I am. It means saying, 'Whatever I am at that moment is just who I am and that's okay. At no point in my life will I ever be perfect.' To fully accept myself, I have to accept and understand the bits of myself that I really don't like and am ashamed for other people to see. They're a part of me, and as long as I'm aware of them, I can act accordingly.

For a long time I felt that I had to belong to a group to feel accepted. Whenever I was with a group, I would become that group, so when I went to school I morphed into a certain group to survive. I got through school by just looking like everybody else. During my teenage years and my early twenties, I used to wonder, 'Well, who am I? I don't know where I fit. Which group do I belong to? The skinheads or the punks or the bikers?'

I was desperate to fit in. I was a chameleon.

Then, as I got older, I realised that I could sit comfortably in all of those groups. I could just be who I was and no one would tell me to bog off. I think that's where we all want to get to, where we genuinely don't give a hoot what people think of us. I just didn't get that concept in my twenties. I looked amazing, but the inner dialogue in my head was like this: 'Should I stand like that or is my tummy sticking out too much or do my boobs look too small and my arse too big and if I lean on this wall I'll look cool. Shall I laugh now? HAHAHA!'

To be more forgiving to ourselves, self-accepting and happy, I have to remind myself all the time that I'm not perfect and that I don't expect perfection from myself or others. I used to really beat myself up when I did something wrong or forgot something important to do with the kids. Trying to be the perfect parent was really important to me and totally exhausting. I'll give you an example.

I went to pick Tilly up on her first day of nursery. I thought I'd left tons of time, but what I didn't know was that on the first day they let them go an hour early, so I was actually late.

As I was driving, I got a call from a girlfriend whose child was at the same nursery.

'Davina, I've got Tilly. I've taken them back to my house because it finished early, so just come and pick her up from mine.'

I burst into tears. I was sobbing like a small child.

'Oh my God, I feel so bad. Is Tilly okay?'

'She's absolutely fine! They're laughing away in the back garden.'

When I got there, my friend opened the front door.

'Oh my God, look at the state of you,' she said. I had snot running down my face, blotchy eyes. 'Come and have a cup of tea before you see Tilly.'

So I had a cup of tea and explained to her that I used to get forgotten as a child and that that feeling has stayed with me for ever. The idea that I might have let my daughter feel like she'd been forgotten, even for one moment, had sent me into a complete tailspin.

My friend took me to the back door.

'Look,' she said. Sitting in the sun on the grass were Tilly and her friend Matilda, husking corn, giggling. ***I realised then that my children are not me***. They are not feeling the same wobbles of insecurity. I show up. If one day I'm late, they know that's out of the norm and that I'll come at some point because I always do. I was never sure if my mum was going to be there. I'm not complaining, that's just how it was. But it shaped me as a mother because it made me want to be there and show up for my own kids, to be perfect.

Luckily, seeing Tilly husking corn brought it home to me that I don't need to be perfect to do a great job as a mother. Now, thank God, if I am late I say, 'Guys, I'm really sorry I'm a bit late.' That's amazing for me, to be able to do that (although, I admit, the rest of the time I'm always ten minutes early).

I've also realised that by always being forgiving to my children when they've done something wrong or they've cocked up, they are like that with me, and it's helped me learn to forgive myself in the same natural way that they forgive me and themselves.

Being more forgiving of myself comes from understanding where my drive to be perfect comes from, accepting who I am right now, warts and all, and being forgiving of other people. I've been very tough on myself in the past, and I've tried to really lighten up and just hug myself a bit more. We all need a little bit of a hug sometimes, don't we? Squeeeeeeeeeeeeeeeeeze.

The void

A lot of people have something painful from their past that leaves a big hole inside them. Mine came from that one golden moment when my mum said, 'I'm coming back in two weeks.' She must have looked after me for the first three-and-a-half years of my life, so to then say 'I'm coming back in two weeks' and never come back, that's hard for a child to comprehend. It is where my fear that anybody I love is going to leave me came from. And I think that everything I did as a child and everything

I did to get into TV or to be famous came from that place of abandonment. I wanted to be famous, I just wanted to get out there and for people to know who I was, because I thought that would be the golden key to make everything okay. 'Be famous, you'll feel better about yourself.' I thought it would fill the void.

This void was in me all through my early childhood and all through my teens. Then I discovered that drink and drugs would temporarily fill the void and that felt like such a relief. For those few hours when I was off my head I would feel okay and, in fact, more than that, I would feel invincible and I'd be dancing on a podium and everybody would be screaming and cheering and I'd be the life and soul of the party. I did that for many years but then it's the same old story, the drugs don't work any more, and you're taking more and more to try and get to that place, that nirvana that you can never return to.

Through years and years and years of working on myself, I have learned to come to terms with that void; but after I stopped taking drugs I would have bet all my money that the thing that was going to fill the hole would be fame, being loved by everybody, to have universal love without drugs. I was sure that would fix me. At the time I would never have said that because I would have felt ashamed to say that I wanted everybody to love me, but I think that was the under-lying hope.

Then, after three years of trying, I finally got the job at MTV and it was such a huge thing for me. I remember think-ing, quite soon afterwards, 'I really, really want my own show.'

After a year or so, MTV offered me a show called *Hanging Out*. It was a live teatime show, really fun, and it was my dream.

I did the first show and everybody was really happy with it, but I had a really weird reaction. I went up to the dressing room and just sobbed. I phoned my sponsor and said, 'I feel awful. I feel so sad.'

'Why? It was great! Why?'

'Because it's not going to do it. It's not going to fix me. I've always thought that this was going to fix me and I don't feel any better.'

'No, it's not going to fix you. Only you can fix you. Nothing from the outside is going to fix you.'

That was a real turning point in my life, realising that outside stuff can't fix you as much as you think it can. Perhaps people will feel it's all very well me saying 'Fame isn't going to fix you' when I'm already famous. 'It's all right for you!' But I'm here, telling you, it's true. I had to fix myself.

My void isn't a hole with a solid bottom that I've slowly been filling over the years until it's full. My void is like a leaky bucket that's constantly draining out, and I have to be vigilant to be sure that I look after myself and top myself up with nurturing and self-love and put an arm round myself, otherwise it just empties out again. I think my fear of abandonment was something that needed attention all the time so that it didn't overwhelm me.

I went to see a hypnotist before filming *Life at the Extreme* because I had to do a deep-sea dive and I was terrified. The hypnotist, Charles, took me back and he realised that my fear of abandonment and my lack of trust were the two things stopping me from feeling safe when diving. He asked me if I was ready to have my fear of abandonment taken away. I was under hypnosis, so he was talking to my subconscious really, but I was awake, I was aware, just very, very relaxed. And do you know what I said? I said, 'No.'

'Why did I say no?' I asked when I came to.

'I don't know. Why do you think you said no?' he said.

'I think I'm frightened that if I have my fear of abandonment taken away, I'm going to be a different person. I've worn this badge for so long it has made me who I am. It's made me understanding, empathetic, a more gentle person and less judgemental of others because I understand what it feels like. What happens if it's taken away? Will I still understand? Will I still be able to relate to people? And will people still be able to relate to me?'

'I'll let you think about that and we can revisit it next week.' All that was in the first session! It gave me a lot to think about.

'Some people need to have a specific sort of personality for their job, a bit like you, and they've had hypnosis to help with something and it hasn't changed them at all,' he said in the second session. 'That's been my experience of helping people, but it's up to you.'

'It's helped them but it hasn't changed them?' I said.

'That's right.'

'Okay.'

So we went back into hypnosis.

'Do you want this fear of abandonment lifted?' he asked.

This time I said, 'Yes.'

'I want you to go back to when you first felt left. When is that?'

I took him back to me in the kitchen at Pippy's house. Mum's gone and I'm drawing at the kitchen table. Pippy's cooking at the Aga and I'm feeling a bit uncomfortable because Mum still hasn't come back. I'm not sure what's happening.

'Get the attention of the younger you,' he said. So I walked behind Pippy and said to my little self, 'Come with me.' It was really weird to see the little me.

'Take her somewhere safe, somewhere you feel comfortable,' he said.

So I took little me by the hand and led her to the big oak tree across the lawn by the gate that led into the fields of the neighbouring farm. When I was young, the farmer let me walk across those fields to a stream that ran along the bottom, and I used to go down there and fish. I loved it there. I sat her down and then I didn't really know what to do with her. I was a bit embarrassed.

'Nurture her, like you would your own children.'

'Come and sit next to me,' I said, putting an arm round her. I gave her a little squeeze, like I would my own kids, and we got talking.

'Are you okay?' I said. The younger me looked confused.

'Tell her it's all going to be okay,' he said. I really started crying at this point. I said, 'I can't tell her it's all going to be okay.'

'Why not?' he said.

'Because it isn't.' I was thinking about all the bad things that happened to me while I was using, the messes that I got myself into, all the drug use, all the people I'd hurt through that.

'But look at you now, Davina.'

That made me cry even more because I suddenly thought, 'Oh good grief, it *is* all going to be okay. I have gone through a really colourful life and it's had big ups and downs but look at me now.' And I looked at the little me, still crying, and said, 'It's all going to be okay. You're going to be okay and your life's going to be colourful and have ups and downs but, I promise you, you will be okay.'

She looked at me and I gave her a really big squeeze. She came in for a nuzzle and I comforted her. I didn't want to let her go.

'You've got to let her go now.'

'I don't want to say goodbye.'

'She needs to go back.'

So we walked across the grass, back to the kitchen, and I sat her down in the chair and stroked her head.

'Bye-bye,' I said. I whispered because Pippy was in the kitchen, but she couldn't see me. Little me waved as I stood at the door.

'How does she look now?' the hypnotist said. 'Look back at her.'

'She looks happy.'

'Have you made her happy?'

'Yeah, she's okay. She knows it's going to be okay.' Then I

smiled to my younger self and left, still crying but not sad, and Charles brought me out of hypnosis. I opened my eyes and felt different.

I still do. It's quite an odd sensation. I'm behaving differently. I am less . . . less complicated. I feel less guilty, generally. I don't feel worried about saying no. I'm a bit more black and white. It's quite tricky for Matthew, I think, because I've had a seismic change. In some ways it's been good for us, because I feel more secure. It's not that I had histrionics before – I'm not a plate-throwing, jibjab-screaming, crying-all-over-the-place type person (although I do like a good cry), but I get less wounded, less frightened. I'm more confident in myself and, as much as I'm really lucky to have Matthew (as all grannies, gay men and girls remind me), he's also bloody lucky to have me! I'm able to see it that way round too now. This shift in me has huge ramifications in my life and, I'm relieved to say, I've done another series of *Long Lost Family* and I can still empathise. Phew!

Never stop working on yourself. You *can't* change other people but you definitely *can* change yourself. That was something I learned when I met Matthew. When I decided to say yes to his proposal, I wondered how I could tell if he was 'the one', out of all the millions of people out there, so I asked myself: 'Do I love the man he is right now? Or am I falling in love with his potential?' I loved him . . . just as he was. When I married him, I had to understand that the chances were that he would never change. So, for example, Matthew wasn't massively domesticated when I met him, so I shouldn't be hugely surprised that he's not massively domesticated now (although he is trying!).

I've changed over the years because I've done work on myself and Matthew has been brilliant at coping with that. I'm not perfect in any way, but there are certain areas where I am better and I imagine I will keep working on myself . . . I enjoy it. All the lessons in this chapter I have learned in the process of filling up my void: sit at the front, make contact, get involved. I think being invisible is a problem in modern-day society. It's very, very easy to be isolated, and that is danger-ous. So make contact. Be seen. Be present. Connect. It's up to us not to wait to be invited, but to make ourselves available. Sometimes that's really frightening to start with, but it works magic.

Learn to say no (it makes your yes mean more)

I still struggle a little bit with this one, though I get waves of being able to do it. *It is very important.*

The way that I learned to say no was when I started going to a 12-step fellowship. I was such an eager member of every meeting that people kept nominating me to fulfil certain roles, like making tea, and because I wanted so badly to fit in and to be liked, and I was so touched that people thought I was nice enough to make the tea, I always said, 'Yes! I'll make the tea.' I was making tea at about eight meetings a week: one a day and on Sundays I had a lunchtime and an evening meeting. The back of my car looked like a supermarket. I had eight different bags for all the different meetings and I had to buy tea and biscuits and milk for everyone, and take the money from the meeting to buy stuff for the next meeting.

After a few weeks I had a bit of a breakdown because it was all just too much responsibility. I had a huge cry and my sponsor said to me, 'You know what? Try saying no.'

'WHAT?!'

'Try saying no.'

It was like she was speaking a different language. I was convinced people wouldn't like me if I said no.

'Give it a go and see what happens. Oh, and maybe you should give up three of your commitments as well.'

'I can't do that! I've only been doing them for a few weeks and I'm supposed to do them for a year. People will hate me because I've taken on a commitment and haven't completed it.'

'Give it a go,' she said.

So, at the end of the next meeting, I put up my hand. 'I'd like to give up my tea commitment. I don't think I can do it any more,' I said, my stomach churning with nerves.

'Okay, no problem. Is there anybody here who would like to do it?'

I couldn't believe that nobody was telling me off or saying that I was a bad person! I was like,

'What? I can say no? This is a thing? Saying no is a thing? This is amazing!'

I learned to say, 'Thank you for the opportunity, I really appreciate it and I understand that you're asking me to do this because you think that I'm an enthusiastic member of this group, but I've already got too many commitments so I have to say no.' I said that at a meeting and people came up afterwards and *praised* me for having guts! I was not just saying no, I was being applauded for saying no. That felt groundbreaking.

Then I went on a no spree. I said no to everything. It was amazing. I was like, 'No! I'm not doing it!'

'Would you like to do this?'

'No! No to everything. No, no, no, no!'

The idea of saying no is awful, but giving yourself permission to do it is empowering. Meghan Trainor learned it from me.

The difficulty I have with saying no at this stage in my life is that I'm having to turn down charity events. I want to say yes because I know it's for a really good cause. I do my fair share for charity, but it never feels like enough. I want to help everybody, and people know that about me, but I'm working hard and I really need to see my husband and my kids. It's a balance and sometimes I *have* to say no. I've also learned that it's much better to say no at the beginning than to say yes, get partway through something and then decide that you can't do it. I've done that before and people get mucho disappointed. Much better to just be strong and say, 'I can't do it.' People nearly always surprise you by saying, 'OK, fine.'

*

Thou shalt not judge, because thou hast also f****d up

I always know when I am not in a good space because a switch goes on in my head called 'judgementalism'. I might look at somebody in a magazine and think, 'Oh my God, look at their hair! Ugh, what are they wearing?' It doesn't make me feel good. In fact, it makes me feel a bit toxic. It's the kind of behaviour that makes me struggle to say 'I love you' in the mirror because I don't like that side of myself. So when I catch myself doing it I ask myself, 'What's going on? What is out of balance? What do I need to do to feel better? Do I need to tell somebody?' Sometimes saying it out loud takes the power out of it.

I think judging is one of the ugliest things we can do to each other because no one knows what is going on in someone else's life; even best friends don't know sometimes. Quite often, because I'm Miss Chatty, I'll get in a taxi and say, 'Ooh, tell me who you've had in! What were they like?' Sometimes the cabbie will reply, 'Oh, I had such-and-such celebrity in the back of my cab the other day. They were a right misery-guts.' And I think of the times I've got into a cab or a car or onto a train after I've had a massive barney with Matthew, or when I've been really worried about my granny or the kids and I'm not bubbly, chatty Davina. I wonder if whoever sees me goes off saying, 'Oh, that Davina, she's a right misery-guts!' We should not judge. EVER.

*

'Two ills don't make a well'

A guy I dated said that. We were both in recovery and had so many issues that we decided we couldn't have a healthy relationship. I thought that was such a funny way of putting it. Sometimes I think you can over-therapise each other. Analysing every feeling was exhausting. As you might be getting from this book, I do a lot of self-analysis . . . that's why I ♥ Matthew. He's just so straightforward to my complicated.

Know that somebody is listening to your prayers

I went to church and sang in the choir every Sunday when I lived with my granny, and we were on first-name terms with the vicar and his wife and children. I'm still friends with them now. When I moved to London, at thirteen, I still went to church on high days and holidays, and now I'm an every-now-and-again Christian. I struggle with the concept of One God or One Belief, because of all the wars in the name of religion, but I do have faith. I have enormous faith in humanity, in people and in prayer.

Before I got married I often visited psychics, because I needed someone to tell me that everything was going to be okay. I went to the College of Psychic Studies in South Kensington and saw this rather amazing guy who, while we were talking, totally freaked me out by mentioning the colourful keyrings in my pocket. How did he know that I had them? They were my NA keyrings. He also told me that my grandfather, Pippy's husband, knew that I prayed every day for strength and courage, even though I wasn't sure who, or what, I was praying to. The psychic asked if I was having a problem with my faith and I struggled to hold back the tears. I admitted that although I understood the need for me to pray to something to stay clean, I didn't know who to pray to. I didn't really know what I was doing. The psychic just said, 'Your grandfather is telling me that he wants you to know your prayers *are* being heard.' Well, that did it. It just made so much sense. What was amazing about it was that it dispensed with the need to put a name or a faith to it. I just know that when the chips are down and I need some help, if I say a little prayer, someone's listening. Having seen my sister die and my granny get older, I'm convinced that as you approach the end of your life, a little bit of faith is a great thing.

Be financially responsible

I am incredibly financially responsible. I'm not frivolous, I don't spend what I haven't got and I'm always thinking, 'Is this an investment or a crazy buying-with-my-heart, ridiculous outgoing that I really shouldn't do?' So I'm quite sensible with money and I owe that entirely to my dad.

With my dad and stepmum we had a nice life. We didn't have much disposable income. They didn't shower me with gifts. I was a thrifty shopper and got really great clothes from second-hand stalls. Going to Top Shop was the treat beyond all treats. I never felt hard done by but I certainly wasn't financially spoilt and I knew that I couldn't rely on my parents for money, and that's a good place to be because it made me stand on my own two feet. At seventeen I got a bank card that was guaranteed by my dad. But at seventeen I was also taking a lot of drugs, clubbing, drinking and spending, spending, spending on the card. I got up to the limit and then went over it by quite a bit. I was getting white envelopes in the post regularly and hoped that if I put them in the bin they would disappear and no one would know.

This weird thing happened inside me each time another white letter arrived: a deep-rooted anxiety took hold, and it grew bigger and bigger and bigger until I'd just see a white envelope and my heart would start palpitating, I felt sick with worry. I just wanted to run away. By that point I knew that the amount of money would be so huge that I would never be able to pay it off and that my dad couldn't pay it off either. I was terrified, really terrified. Whenever I see adverts for companies that do high-interest loans for people like me, when I was in debt, it makes me so angry because all you do is get yourself further into debt. Debt could have driven me to do something really bad, because I felt like I had nowhere to go.

Thank God my dad had guaranteed my bank account because they finally wrote *him* a letter saying, 'We've been trying to contact your daughter, to no avail. She's got £3,500 worth of debt, and we'd like her to come in to talk it through.'

When Dad got this letter he came and talked to me about it. He didn't shout. He taught me that no matter what happened I could always go to him and we would sort it out together.

I wept with relief at my secret being out. He then did the very best thing he could have done. He told me to make an appointment with the bank manager. I was terrified they would shout at me but he reassured me that this sort of thing happens all the time but that I needed to sort it out, and that they'd be pleased I'd gone to see them. I didn't understand that but I went anyway, on my own, and we came up with terms whereby I would pay them back at £20 a week until I could start paying more. It took me about four years to pay it off. I had no debit card and absolutely no credit card, just a cheque book, for four years so I could only withdraw cash by cheque from the bank, which is an almighty pain in the jacksy, but I was so grateful. The minute I paid it off I got another £3,500 loan and bought a car. I must have been about twenty-two or twenty-three.

This lesson about money was fantastic. Dad didn't make me go and see the bank manager alone because he was mean. He wanted me to learn that if I could get myself into a pickle, I needed to be able to get myself out of it too. But he showed me what to do and how to do it and I really thank him for making me much more financially responsible than I would have been otherwise.

*

Gratitude keeps you positive

Gratitude unlocks the fullness of life. It turns what we have into enough, and more. It turns denial into acceptance, chaos to order, confusion to clarity.

Melody Beattie

I love this quote.

I had a tricky childhood and in my teens I found relationships quite hard, but

from the minute I got clean I got grateful and that gratitude keeps me positive.

I think the fact I can put a positive spin on everything is because I'm always grateful for where I'm at and I try to never, ever take anything that I have for granted.

Five ways to get an 'attitude of gratitude':

1. Write a gratitude diary every night. List at least three things you are grateful for – more will soon come. If you're stuck, you can start with things like 'running water', 'trees', 'a bed to lie on' and so on.

2. Have a big glass jar in your kitchen and a notebook and pencil nearby. Every time you think of something to be grateful for, write it down and pop it in the jar. Get the family to join in, and read them out on a special day like

Christmas Eve, New Year's Day . . . This is particularly lovely if you have expressed gratitude to someone who is reading the notes with you!

3. Write a letter or an email to someone you feel grateful to, even if you haven't been in contact for years. You don't have to send it for it to work.

4. Say 'thank you' to people at every opportunity – a door held open, a driver letting you pass, a helpful person at the bank – any chance to thank another person will add to your own sense of gratitude in life.

5. Be grateful even for difficulties. They often show the invaluable lessons you need to learn in order to move into even greater happiness and gratitude. I think my most valuable life lessons have come out of a problem or dark time in my life.

The power of a smile and a hug

I smile at people during 12-step meetings. I try to smile a lot as I know how it felt when I was new. A few years later I bumped into someone who said, 'You smiled at me four years ago and it kept me in that room.' I had forgotten, but he said, 'I'll never forget you for it.' Isn't that amazing? The power of a smile. And other people have done that for me. It's so powerful when somebody smiles at you.

It's the same with hugging. I love hugging (you may already know that!). A hug can speak louder than words and sometimes only a hug will do. They can heal a million woes. A hug says, 'I really care, I'm feeling for you.'

I generally hug for a little bit too long, although I have got much better at judging when somebody's uncomfortable with hugging. I did a show called *Reborn in the USA* with a singer from my childhood called Elkie Brooks. I got a note before the show started saying that Elkie did not like to be touched. I worked hard to respect her space, but it was funny how difficult I found it.

I was extremely pleased to read recently that there is a significant therapeutic value to a hug that lasts for twenty seconds or more. Oxytocin levels in the body rise and that makes you feel more relaxed. Hugs reduce blood pressure, improve immunity to infection, help children develop into less stressed adults, and much more besides. I thought, 'There you go!' I must have known somehow that my uncomfortably long hugs, even if somebody's patting me to release, are making them and me feel a whole lot better. The exchange can be mutual. I've definitely been in lovely hugs where I've received and given at the same time.

Stick with the winners

I have noticed in life that there are givers and takers. The other day I heard a fantastic expression: 'radiators and drains'. I hope I'm a radiator and that I give and don't just take.

There's a great saying in NA which is really simple: 'Stick with the winners.' I think that's a great lesson. Stick with the people who make you feel good when you're with them and avoid emotional vampires – they will just suck you dry. They love a positive person and you must protect yourself. I'm not saying don't help people. Help lots of people. But there are some people who are beyond helping because *they don't want to be helped*; they enjoy swimming in their pool of negativity. Avoid at all cost!

Sit at the front

I learned so many life skills by getting clean, but a fundamental one is that if you want to learn something, or, in my case, if I wanted to get and stay well, I needed to sit at the front. It was tempting to sit at the back and gossip to people, to make friends and laugh and giggle, but I knew I couldn't go back to how things were and that I had to sit in the front row and be on board. I think this idea applies to a lot of things in life. If you want to learn, change a habit, grow, you can't just sit and giggle with your friends, you can't just think about being popular and commenting from the sidelines. You've got to sit in the front row and be part of life.

*

Learn to listen

OMG, this is something that really takes practice!

My Uncle Simon and his wife, Niamh, live in Australia, so we don't get to see them very often, but we absolutely cherish our visits with or from them. They are the sorts of people everybody really, really likes. Matthew and I have analysed Simon and Niamh quite a lot. We've asked ourselves, 'What is it that makes them so special?' We both agree it's because they really listen. You know that they're listening because they give you amazing eye contact, they're engaged, and they ask you exactly the right questions. Uncle Simon was in market research, which makes absolute sense, because he always knows what to ask, he takes time, and he only ever turns the conversation round to himself if he's got a great example of something to tell you.

Sometimes, when I was newly clean and still full of self-obsession, I'd spend literally a whole meeting thinking about what was I going to say, so even when I wasn't speaking I wasn't really listening either. My sponsor noticed that I was talking in every meeting and said, 'Why don't you try not talking in a couple of meetings and just listen?' This advice freed me from the obsession of thinking about what I was going to say and I suddenly started hearing all these fantastic golden nuggets of recovery that I had been missing before. After that, I only spoke if something really struck me as useful to say or that I needed to share.

I've learned over time that listening is an artform that's vital if I want to have brilliant relationships with people. I was definitely rubbish at it when I was younger, but now I feel that not only am I listening, I'm really enjoying hearing. I'm interested.

Long Lost Family is a programme where listening is more important than speaking. I do more listening in that programme than I do speaking, and people value feeling heard. It's taught me not to immediately interject when someone stops speaking. Sometimes I will let there be complete silence after somebody has spoken, because what they have just told me deserves a respectful pause. The long pauses sometimes get cut out of the finished programme but I still do them, because the person speaking needs to know that I have heard them and am taking the time to let their words sink in.

My guidelines for listening are:

1. Look the person in the eye and don't let yourself get distracted. Focus on that person.

2. Try not to think, 'I could ask them this ... Maybe I could ask them that ... I don't agree with that!' while they're talking, because if you're doing that, you're not really listening. If somebody's telling you something difficult or painful, just let it breathe afterwards. Give them time to think it through. They might need the space to process information and by jabbing in with advice you're not letting

them process their words. That's definitely something I learned from *Long Lost Family*.

3. Don't interrupt.

It's important that everybody gets a listen, especially children. I use a lot of what I've learned in the fellowship with our kids. I try not to interrupt, I let them finish what they're saying, I give them time to breathe; if they've dropped a massive piece of information and I just want to go, 'WHAT?', I try not to. I let it breathe. Kids deserve to be heard just as much as we do.

Everybody needs to be heard. Me too.

When Matthew and I argue it's often because I feel he hasn't heard me. He'll listen, but he might not be hearing and I'll feel that half his brain is still at work or on the ultimate fighting he's going to watch in five minutes. Then I say, 'I really need you right now to be here, hearing me.'

Matthew and I have great chats after a little blow-up that hasn't been resolved. We've gone our separate ways and then, two days later, we come back to the same topic but we're calm. The kids have gone to bed, the dogs are asleep, we're in the kitchen, there's no TV or phone, and we just sit and look at each other. That is when stuff gets resolved. Listening, eye contact, respect, boundaries, calm. That's when the magic happens ... And if I look at Matthew for more than thirty seconds I find him so attractive I go all funny ... in a nice way!!

*

Don't let your past define you

Sometimes we let our pasts define us and sometimes we let other people define us by our pasts, which is probably worse. I got an amazing troll the other day when somebody wrote, 'Who's looking after your kids while you're doing a shit job on this show with your nose which is as big as a ski-jump, you ex-junkie slag?' I blocked them, obvs, and at the same time actually laughed because I could tell that they must have really thought that insult through, I mean really crafted it, but I didn't let it touch me. You know, I love my nose. My nose is one of my most favourite parts of my body. I'm sure when people see me in the street it's my nose that they recognise (or see first . . . hee hee).

Jon Snow said once, 'Davina, you really have got the most beautiful nose.' You have no idea how much that meant to me, Mr Snow. Gorgeous man.

'Ex-junkie slag?' I will not let another person's negative opinion define me. I've broken out from that. All my friends know that drugs are a part of my past but not my present.

I think, today, we're all a bit more accepting of people's failures. I'm hoping it's because people like me come out and admit that **I was once a mess but I choose not to be a mess any more, and so I'm not. If I can do it, you can do it. It's that simple**. But if you let it define you, if you become that person, you'll never get out of that cycle of negative thought and it will keep you imprisoned. If you keep thinking, 'This is what I am, I am a junkie, I am a thief, I am a bad person, I was born bad ...' – rubbish! We all have the power to change. We can all be different. Sometimes it's really, really, really scary to make that step because without drugs, who am I? If I'm not dancing on a podium, being hysterical, being up all night, being the last one to leave, who am I? I'm nothing. That's rubbish. I'm a better person now (and I still dance all night).

Sometimes you need a bit of help moving away from your past, but there is so much help out there. I think talking to somebody else is powerfully healing. They don't have to be a counsellor or a hypnotist. ***Keeping something to yourself is toxic. Share it with someone*** – I'll repeat that a lot in this book, and look forward.

One day at a time

I'd be telling you a bit of a porky pie if I said I'd learned to entirely 'live in the now', but I'm striving on a daily basis to achieve it. Living in the present, or in the moment, is something everybody's talking about right now; they're prescribing mindfulness on the NHS, we're all reading mindfulness books (or buying them anyway). 'Just for today', or taking one day at a time, is a brilliant idea for an addict, because tomorrow's too much to think about. Tomorrow's too big and next week, next year, is too much. Even now, when I don't keep it in the moment, I can get very anxious.

As an addict you're not thinking 'Oh my gosh, if I stay clean for a couple of months I might be able to move out of my dad and stepmum's,' or 'If I stay clean I can start working at MTV ...' It's too much to think about that.

I'd like to say that I can tell you how to live in the present, how to *be* in the present, but all I can tell you is that I'm on a bit of a journey and I'll write that book when I know how.

Top tips to survive being dumped

Been dumped? Yup, me too – it's crappy. Here's how to get through it.

Firstly, listen to Meghan Trainor's 'No' really loudly over and over again until you totally absorb that 'brush-off' attitude she gets so brilliantly in that song. Obvs that wasn't around when I was being dumped, wish it was ... If it's come as a total surprise that you've been dumped, ***don't show it***. When somebody completely shocks me, I've generally found that the best thing to do is to behave completely unfazed and unflabbergasted and then find the nearest cupboard or toilet or small area where you can go 'ARGGGGH!'

Right, so you've been singing along with Meghan Trainor. Then you go to the hairdresser. Get your hair zhuzhed. Or change it, or dye it, or get your roots done. Do all the things that you got a little bit slack about when you were comfortable with your ex. Wax your legs, go to the gym, paint your nails or your shed (not a euphemism), pluck your eyebrows. Own yourself. Reclaim your body. You're not pimping up or dressing up for anybody else, you're doing this *for you*. (BTW – please don't think I ever did what a bloke told me to do – quite the opposite. If a boyfriend said to me, 'Oh, you should work out,' or 'You should do this to your hair ...' it would always make me want to do the absolute opposite. 'Oh, you should train.' I'd spend the afternoon on the sofa watching films.)

Sometimes we lose ourselves in relationships. I've done that before and when it ended I decided to do a massive Davina overhaul. I'd lose weight. It would just fall off, I'd just be really depressed. Then I'd start exercising and I'd start to feel amazing. And my boyfriends would want me back because I'd suddenly become more confident. When you're needy and insecure, they run a mile.

I've got quite good at feeling amazing without being dumped. Perhaps being with the right person helps to do that?

Once you're feeling fit and gorgeous again, get a friend and sign up to a dating website. Do it with a friend because it makes something that can sometimes feel a bit tragic into a fun event. Have a laugh. Have a glass of wine (or coke zero) and be honest. Being honest is really important. Don't write that you're twenty-two, tall and blonde unless it's true!

The last thing? Don't mope about listening to sad music. Stay busy. You're allowed to wallow in it for a bit, but then pick yourself up, because, even if you're faking feeling happy, that might turn into real happy. Go out, go out, go out. You'll feel happy in the end. Literally, that's my number-one way of dealing with everything. Fake it to make it.

If you've been dumped and you have kids, obviously I have no direct experience, but my advice would still be that you can look after yourself, get your hair done, exercise with the children, make yourself feel good. What's going to be important is to show them that, even though you've split up with someone, you're not letting it destroy you. You might howl into your pillow at night, but they don't need to see that. You split up with somebody and you don't let it ruin your life.

Dogs really are man's best friend

Sometimes, I'll be talking to one of my dogs (in human language, I don't speak dog yet. I'm working on it) and it'll look at me and I'll know that it's got what I'm saying. It's probably due to intonation, my expression, the hormones or pheromones I'm giving off, and other things we don't even understand yet, but they get it. They understand.

Animals have always been really important to me, especially dogs. Much more than just being the animal that you can go on a long walk with, or that's nice and warm to snuggle up next to on the sofa, they have another level of intuition and sensitivity that really does make them man's best friend. We've seen dogs do amazing things for people with disabilities or learning difficulties. They can heal grief. They can heal loneliness. Animals are very healing. The unconditional love you get from a dog is unlike any other love you get from **anybody**. They don't ask anything of you and they give so much. How anybody could be cruel to a dog I just don't get. They feel like we do.

Dogs have always been there for me in my time of need. They are unbelievable creatures with powers that go way beyond their cuteness. One of our dogs, Bo, is particularly sensitive and whenever I'm feeling a little bit funny she's always the one who comes to my side.

I'll never forget the time when my sister, Caroline, was sick. In the last three days before she died she went to sleep, and I knew that she wasn't going to wake up again, so I kept a bedside vigil and Bo stayed with me the whole time. She's a bouncy dog normally, and full of energy, but she stayed so quiet and calm, because she knew that that was what was needed.

The same thing happened a little while ago when Pippy had a mini-stroke. I got a call to come quickly. So I ran to Pippy's cottage and the dogs followed me, but instead of coming in, they kept running up and down outside, agitated and anxious. They could sense what was going on.

I got my first dog when I was eight. I remember going in to see my great-grandma in her granny flat with Pippy. She had a puppy on her knee and I was so excited! 'Grandma, you've got a puppy!' And she said, 'It's not my puppy, it's your puppy.' I don't think I've ever felt joy like it. I was running around on the grass with my puppy, just crying with happiness. That was my first proper dog, Geordie.

When I was living in London with my stepmum and dad we didn't have a dog, but I got my own dog when I was twenty-seven. She was called Rosie and had been very badly treated before she arrived at Battersea Dogs Home. Every time I lifted anything quickly, she'd cower. But she was incredibly intuitive. Whenever I was sad, Rosie would always be right next to me or put her head on my lap.

It was through walking Rosie that I met Matthew. At that time Rosie (sorry about this) slept in my bed. Not on it, but in it, with her head on the pillow and her paws on the duvet. She was a cross between a Rottweiler and a Labrador. She was big.

When I met Matthew, Rosie had to not only get out of the bed, but out of the bedroom. She was not happy about that at all. Matthew has asthma triggered by dog hair, so I had to deep-clean my entire bedroom so that Matthew didn't touch dog hair, otherwise he'd never come and stay with me.

Rosie got ousted to the corridor until Matthew and I bought our first home, when she got ousted to downstairs. She had to live with Chloe, Matthew's dog, and Rosie did not like Chloe. Rosie was the alpha dog and poor Chloe, a boxer, wanted to be Rosie's friend, but she wasn't having it. Poor Rosie had gone from being in bed with me, head on my pillow, to downstairs with an annoying dog (to her . . . We adored Chloe, obvs).

Then, when we moved to the country, we had this lovely lady Jill who used to help me with cleaning the house. She'd look after Rosie and Chloe if we went on holiday, and they were allowed in Jill's bedroom, on the bed, wherever they wanted to go. She lived just a few doors up and, after about two years, Rosie would run to Jill's house and sit on her doorstep. It broke my heart but I knew Jill was giving her the closeness she was no longer getting from me, so after this happened a few times I said, 'Jill, how do you feel about taking Rosie on, because I think she wants to be with you?'

'I'd love that!' she said.

'And Rosie'll love it because she gets to be in your bed.'

So Rosie left me and went to live with Jill. I was heartbroken but I knew it was the best thing for her.

Our dogs now are very different. They're outside dogs. They're allowed to wander the house but none of them have ever been allowed upstairs. Even so, I totally feel that they are part of the family and I would *never* be without a dog. If you don't have one, you can borrow a dog for walks and even for a weekend. See the website www.borrowmydoggy.com

3

Careers Advice

Be as determined as a mosquito!

It took *three* years to get my job at MTV. To work there was my dream and I was laser-focused on it. I'd say to people, 'I'm going to work at MTV,' and they'd all be like, 'Yeah, whatevs, everybody wants to work at MTV. Join the queue.' I'd look at them and think, 'No, but I really *am* going to.' I wouldn't say that out loud, of course, I'd sound really cocky, but I thought it!

At the time I was working as a booker at Models 1 and in nightclubs to make ends meet; but I would see VJs and think, 'That would be the *best job ever*!' The average age of people working at MTV was twenty-six – how cool is that?! I started making short films and putting them together for audition tapes. Oh my God, I made the *War and Peace* of audition tapes.

My first one was called 'The Last Man on Earth', in which the person behind the camera is the last man on earth and I play six different women, all with some burning agenda concerning the man. MTV clearly thought I was bonkers but kind of interesting. They didn't give me a job, they said I wasn't what they were looking for, but I thought:

'Ha! you just don't know that you want me yet.'

I kept going back again and again and again and when somebody said, 'Look, please stop phoning me,' I'd say, 'Sure, if you give me someone else's number to call instead.'

I did that for three years and I'm convinced that fate made me wait that long because when I **was** finally invited to audition I'd been clean from drink and drugs for six months. If I'd auditioned while I was using, I would have cocked it up for sure, and that would have been that.

On the day of the screen test they sent a taxi for me. I thought I had arrived! I remember the journey to MTV, looking out of the window, and screaming in my head, 'I'm in a TAXI!! This is the life!' I absorbed every second of it but at the same time I was thinking, 'This is three years of pent-up **wanting** and I get *one chance* at it. *Oh my God, this is it*. DON'T COCK IT UP.'

They asked me to go with a crew to review Rose & Jim's Restaurant in Camden, and all went well until I started talking about the famous people who had eaten there. In the window were newspaper cuttings with photos, and one of them was of a sumo wrestler. I started to read his name but I couldn't pronounce it! So I just made it up. 'Look, Konishikuku ate here!' I said, with a very straight face.

I heard nothing for *three months* and all I could think of was how stupid I must have looked trying to pronounce that name. When the phone call finally came, it was Alan Howard telling me I'd got the job. I went ballistic, screaming, jumping up and down, unable to speak. It felt FANTASTIC. After I'd calmed down, he invited me in to meet the big cheese, Brian Diamond. I asked Brian why it had taken them so long to tell me. 'If I'm honest,' he said, 'it was a toss-up between you and another girl.' I asked him why he chose me and he said, 'I just couldn't stop laughing at you trying to pronounce the sumo wrestler's name.' That's when I realised that being myself is okay. So, since then, I've made a career out of making a bit of a plonker of myself and trying not to care too much because some people seem to like it.

Getting that job was probably the proudest moment in my life. Everywhere I went people said, 'Bloody hell, Davina, well done,' because I had told everybody I knew, and a lot of people I didn't really know, that I was going to work at MTV, so when it actually happened they were thrilled for me. It was a *Sliding Doors* moment. Suddenly I was on a different path.

So the lesson it taught me is this:

If you really believe in something, if you really want something, if you love someone, don't give up at the first hurdle – put your whole life into it.

As Anita Roddick says in the film *1 Giant Leap* in her chat about solo activism: 'If you think you're too small to make a difference, you've never been to bed with a mosquito.' I think that's brilliant! So whenever I meet a young person who wants to be a presenter and they say, 'Well, I've been to a couple of places and they turned me down,' I say, 'WHAT?! Are you just going to accept that? If you want something, don't be British about it and get all embarrassed. Be as persistent as a mosquito until you get it!'

Never burn your bridges

When I worked on *Big Brother*, every year I would have a different runner (someone on the first rung of the TV production ladder who is sent on errands – the good ones move fast and you know they won't be runners for long!) and I would always try and get to know them a bit: what do you want to do? Where do you want to go? What area of TV do you want to work in? I could always tell the ones who were going to go far. There was a runner called Tom on *Got to Dance* – OMG he was unbelievable! He was always lightly sweating because he ran *everywhere* with a backpack containing the biggest thermos you've ever seen so that if anybody ever wanted a hot cup of tea, outside, inside, anywhere, he could provide it. Tom was just so *on it* which made me rather sad because I knew that he would only be my runner for a nanosecond. He would be producing before you knew it. He was always two steps ahead of everybody else.

I don't understand anybody who looks down on the people they work with, especially in TV, because that's who's going to be your boss one day. Tom is now producing and in four years' time he'll probably be a big boss. So just be nice to people on the way up because you'll meet them on the way back down. P.S. When I started in TV I met a researcher called Duncan who went on to run ITV and gave me the job on *Got to Dance*!

Fake it till you make it!

'Faking it till you make it' is what I do when I'm sad, when I catch myself wallowing, or when I'm feeling anything *but* showy and have to go on TV. I fake the feeling I want to summon up until something shifts and I start to feel it for real.

After my sister died there were times when I really, *really* didn't want to get in front of the camera. Just before I went on I would fake feeling happy and after about fifteen minutes I would find that I was actually having quite a good time and I could present the rest of the show genuinely excited about it.

I fake confidence too, when it deserts me. I went to a Channel 4 drinks party the other night and as I walked up the steps on my own, a wave of insecurity hit me. I was thinking, 'Why have I come here on my own? I'm completely insane. I'm not going to know anybody. Why am I wearing this?' When I walked in, even though I've been in this business for twenty-four years, I knew no one. In desperation I went up to a woman with a baby and started talking to the baby! Then I realised that I must look mad and walked off again. In my head, I was screaming, 'Help me! Please!' I can't even drink to ease the pain, which is lucky because it would have been a prime time to get absolutely mullered.

I was standing there, enormously awkward, when I saw a bloke with big muscles and a beard, also on his own.

'Hi. You've got very big muscles – bet you work out,' I said. It was the brashest thing I could think of with which to start a conversation. Turns out he was feeling awkward too and didn't know anybody either. He was former SAS and had only just signed a deal with Channel 4 and wanted to celebrate. We had a brilliant chat and when people we knew started arriving, we could introduce each other to everyone. What was an agonis-ing, excruciating twenty minutes ended up being a wonderful evening, all because I faked enough confidence to start a conversation.

Faking it works for all ages. My son was struggling after the holidays, not wanting to go back to school or me to go back to work. But after a week of him feeling sad I said, 'Right, today I want you to go in and fake feeling happy and see if halfway through lunchtime, when you're playing with all your friends, you start to really feel happy.' And he did. He faked feeling okay and joined his friends playing football and felt much better.

It's a powerful tool, pretending.

*

Give more than is expected

Our family motto is 'Give more than is expected.' There wasn't actually a moment in my life that made me come up with this phrase: I read it in a book, but it was like somebody had smashed a pickaxe through my forehead. It made such sense to me. I thought, 'That is the best life lesson ever!' It rings true in every single area of my life. I've written it down all over the place and I keep drumming it into the kids and myself.

I like to think that I've always tried to give more than is expected; going that extra mile for somebody stands you in really good stead. In my work, I know that people think that I'm an OK person to work with because I try never to complain. There are a lot of other people on a show doing a much tougher job than I am, working the same hours, and it's harder for them. I always try and come in with a smile on my face. If ever I wasn't giving 120 per cent I think people would know that it's not because I'm bolshie or think I'm better than other people or I've lost touch with reality, but because I'm not well or I'm upset about something. I'm pretty sure I've been asked back on things because I've given them a bit of extra time, or I'll see a new director who's struggling and she'll be looking at the clock and I'll say, 'Don't worry, I've got time.' I only ever tried to rush home from work when the kids were really small.

'Give more than is expected' has become part of the fabric of our family. In a funny kind of way, it's a selfish act. Giving more than is expected makes you feel just as good as it does everybody else.

We were in a hotel the other day and the barman gave us a drink. We were abroad, he had no idea who I was, but he said to my son, 'Hey, fella! I've got some cards behind the bar. Do you want to play with a pack of cards?' And then he suggested a really nice fruit cocktail that Chester might enjoy drinking. When we left Chester said, 'He gave more than was expected.' Chester had noticed that this guy had made an effort to make *his* time at the bar as much fun as it had been for Matthew and me. It's lovely that he noticed that someone else gave more than was expected. It stops him expecting stuff and it makes him realise that people go out of their way to help us have a nice day, which in turn makes us more polite because we're grateful; so in a million different ways this one phrase was one of the best things that ever jumped off a page at me.

Be nice to newbies: they'll never forget it

Denzel Washington taught me this lesson (God, that sounds cool, doesn't it?).

When I was working on *Good Stuff* with Rowland Rivron, the only way that we could get to interview the really big-name guests was to pick them up from their hotel in a limo and drive them to their function. I'd interview them on the way.

I was quite new to celebrities at the time. I'd done MTV for four years by then (I was twenty-nine), but I felt very at home with musicians and didn't really see them as 'celebrities'. Film stars though, that was different. I was a bit starstruck with them.

Good Stuff was one of my first terrestrial TV programmes and I was a bit nervous about that too. So we picked up Denzel Washington in the limo and I was quite on edge I had no idea what he was going to be like and I'd always rather loved him in movies. He was doing interviews for the release of *Training Day*. He got into the back of the car and I tried to be myself. I said, 'Okay? Are you okay to start?'

'Yes, I'm fine,' he said.

I asked him the first question and he leaned over and touched my knee and looked as if he was going to say something but not in response to my question.

'Oh my God, what's happening?' I thought.

'Are you nervous?' he said.

'Yes, I am,' I said, rather awkwardly.

'Okay,' he said, 'let's both wind down our windows –' we were on Park Lane at the time, '– stick our heads out and scream really loudly and then come back in.'

I started giggling. 'Okay,' I said.

'Let's do it now,' he said. So we opened our windows, stuck out our heads and screamed really loudly. I closed the window, looked at him and started laughing.

'Do you feel better? he said.

'I do. I do!'

'Good. Shall we start again?'

I just wanted to lick his face and say, 'I know this is inappropriate, but I think I love you.'

I didn't do either of those things, but it was wonderful to meet someone I'd always loved in movies and discover that he was the nicest, kindest, sweetest person. I'll never forget that. And he gave me such a good interview.

Since then, if I ever meet somebody I can see is a bit nervous, I always try to do something to break the ice like pulling a face, cracking a joke, taking them to one side to have a whisper, making them tea, because I remember what being nervous feels like and how much it meant to me that Denzel Washington didn't just let me carry on with the interview but cared enough to help me feel better.

When I *feel* sassy, I *deliver* sassy

I used to be a great believer in underplaying myself. I wouldn't make too much of an effort or wear make-up; I did the natural, casual look all the time. When I started working with Garnier, eleven years ago, I was about to leave for a meeting with them in London, wearing jeans and a baggy T-shirt with a pair of trainers, when I said to myself, 'Given that this is a business meeting, should I businessify my look a bit? Maybe lose the puffa jacket? Have I got a smarter top?'

'Hmmm,' I thought, 'I'm going to give that a go.' I swapped my trainers for a pair of boots with high heels, found a T-shirt that fitted me, dumped the stay-alive-on-the-north-face-of-the-Eiger puffa and put on a blazer, a scarf and a little bit of make-up. What was interesting was that I *felt* different. I was still in my jeans but I went into the meeting feeling sassy and when I *feel* sassy I *deliver* sassy!

I've also learned to wear what I like. I've spent such a long time trying to be things that I'm not, like trying to be really girly or wearing clothes that don't quite suit me. It's not that other people expect it of me, but *I* think I should be girly, so I almost put it on myself. Now I realise that extreme girliness is just not very me. I do my own version of feminine.

When you go out and you don't feel right in what you're wearing, it is so uncomfortable and humiliating; you want to disappear in a corner. It's made me realise that you have to wear what you feel good in even if it's not the kind of thing that *anybody* else will be wearing at that occasion. Just go with it.

That confidence has come only in the last ten years. I've embraced the look I feel most comfortable with, which is definitely at the masculine end of the spectrum, but slightly feminised. So I love wearing trousers and suits but make them look pretty with a heel (though not when I'm wandering around at home), or with a bit of jewellery or a scarf or something. When I look at pictures of myself when I was a teenager, I wore exactly what I wanted and was a total tomboy, always in shorts or trousers. So it's about embracing your own style but subtly making it work for different occasions with something a bit businessy, glamorous or pretty.

It's not that I don't make mistakes. I've made millions of

fashion mistakes, but what's really funny is that when every-body else says, 'What were you thinking?' I'm there saying, 'I don't know what you're talking about. I look smoking hot!' Sometimes I think I've got some weird body dysmorphia. Everybody else is looking at me and seeing some deeply unfashionable old woman and I'm seeing Elle Macpherson. I'm often in the 'What was she thinking?' pages of a magazine. But care? Me? No.

I would only take something off if I myself felt uncomfort-able in it and I never think 'Am I too old for this?' The other day I was wearing a hairband with a big fabric white skull and huge black bow.

'Mum, isn't that a bit, you know . . .?' my daughter said.

'What? I said.

'You know . . . Mutton?'

'Mmmm . . . I feel okay in it,' I said, and it stayed on. I feel okay in the hairband with the big bow on it, but I'd only wear shorts or bare my midriff on holiday. I'll still crack out a jump-suit (even though most people think they're only for the young), because it's how *you* feel that matters, not the judge-ments of others.

Now let's talk about underwear. I got into hot water recently because I said that, being half-French, I always like to wear matching underwear. I feel a bit out of kilter if my underwear doesn't match. Most of the time I wear extremely practical underwear from M&S in plain colours: black and black, white and white, beige and beige, pink and pink. But if I'm going for a meeting where I really want to make a good impression or I want to kick some butt, I wear amazing underwear because it makes me feel great. It doesn't have to be nipple-less or crotch-less or something extreme, just something that makes me feel pretty. I think that when we've had kids and we're exhausted and in the middle of the drudgery of life, underwear is the first thing that goes because we can't be arsed. I've been there. But when your underwear goes grey, CHUCK IT. Everybody can afford new underwear now and again. Sometimes I get it from Agent Provocateur, which is expensive, but often I get it from Marks & Spencer, or Victoria's Secret, which is not. Something in a pretty colour with a bit of lace does the trick. Contrary to popular belief, when I wear sexy underwear it isn't for my husband. I used to wear sexy underwear when I was single. It's for *me* and it's how it makes *me* feel. I feel empowered and in control and strong when I wear nice underwear. I feel calm and relaxed when I've got a matching colour on. I love walking through Charing Cross train station and knowing I've got some really, really sexy underwear on and nobody else knows. That's fun!!

Be honest

A really valuable lesson I've learned in TV, which has helped me in life in general, is that you've got to be honest about stuff that's going on even if it's a bit contentious or not brilliant.

I value honesty as much as fidelity.

There's that lovely phrase 'honest to a fault', and to me it means that you are always honest, even when it's to your own detriment; even when it means people might ridicule you or dislike you, you're going to be honest anyway. That is something that I massively admire in people and value highly. I find it hugely disarming when someone is really honest; I think, 'Oh, right, okay, so we're gonna have it like that? Amazing!'

If honesty is something that you hugely admire and value and think is amazing, it makes being honest with other people a bit easier. So, for example, a really small place to practise total honesty is when cancelling things like dinners or playdates. I've had times when the kids have been really reluctant to go round to someone's house – not because they don't like them, they just want to stay at home. You know that if you insist they go they're going to have the worst time ever and they'll be crying and ruin it for everybody. In those cases, I phone up and say, 'I don't know what's wrong. They're having a funny moment.' I don't say, 'They've got an auntie coming round.'

You can't go anywhere with the truth. The truth is the truth and it stops right there. I've told you the truth. There's nothing I can do about it. It's the truth.

With a lie, there's always somewhere to go with it, and that's eventually to the truth!

If we tell a lie and get found out, it's the worst thing ever! People feel a lack of respect for us, or maybe, even worse, pity. Oh! Oh! It's horrific!! In the same way, there is massive respect for somebody when they're painfully honest and tell us something even though it's to their detriment.

Dishonesty, especially where you're spinning a whole web of it, means you need to have a very good memory to remember everybody you're lying to and how; you will make yourself sick because it's like a blackness in your veins that will go into your very core. It comes from fear. *Honesty takes huge courage.*

And I'm not talking about the sort of thing that often happened on *Big Brother*, when someone says, 'Well, I'm just being honest,' when they're slagging off someone's appearance or their boyfriend or the way they are. Don't slag off something under the premise of being 'honest' . . . That's just cruelty. It's mean.

However, when someone is a very, very, very good friend and has been for a very very long time then sometimes you can point something out that you don't like. You can say, 'Look, that dress just doesn't suit you. You're so pretty, try a different colour.'

My best friend Sarah and I are *so* honest with each other, about everything. I bought her a bag once and was so excited about it. I thought it was going to be the absolute perfect bag for her, but she said, 'Look, I love it, but I like the other colour. Do you mind if I swap it?' I didn't mind at all. I just love her honesty. I'd much rather she had the bag she loved. Once there was something going on with me that made me be a bit hard on her. She said, 'I think you've been really hard on me and I don't know what's going on.' Her honesty made me own up to what I'd done, because she was right. I called her back and said, 'I'm really sorry. I don't know what's wrong with me.'

Being honest with the press is the same. Sometimes a journalist will come up to me and say, 'But you said in an interview fifteen years ago that you . . .' and I'll reply, 'I've changed my mind.' We're allowed to change our opinions and how we feel about things. My truth from when I was thirty is going to be very different to my truth when I'm forty-five.

Sometimes a storm will blow up in the press or on social media over something that feels untrue to me. Press officers always say, 'It will just go away if you don't say anything,' but sometimes it's important to tell my side of the story. What's amazing about social media is that we all, not just famous people, have an opportunity to get out there and tell the truth about a situation. There was a story I call 'Pantgate', that blew up over something I said about wearing matching underwear, as I've mentioned before. There was a whole torrent of debate about whether I was undermining the sisterhood by admitting that I like wearing matching underwear, or was showing true feminist credentials because I wore it for myself and not for Matthew. I just got out there and wrote a blog to say what I really meant and to put back in context the words that had been taken out and blown up into something that felt untrue. My press agent didn't want me to, he said the story would disappear, but I could see it blowing up and I wanted to get my point across. I'm glad I did, and after that it just went away.

I try to be honest all the time, even if it means bringing up things that are very complicated, sensitive and difficult for people to talk about. I will just talk about them anyway, which isn't always popular, but I think it's important.

When Caroline was dying, it felt right not to hide her illness from our children. I never told them that they couldn't go and see her. I *always* let them know when she'd got a step worse and kept them informed. Right up until the last minute, Chester was nipping in to see Caroline. She looked really, really poorly but I think the kids appreciated the open door policy and I know she did.

The kids all went to the funeral, even though some people questioned the wisdom of that. Chester was incredible and brought us much-needed light in what was a time of real anguish. He was five and asked wonderfully normal questions like 'Is Caroline in the box? Where's the box going to go?' When the coffin goes it's heartbreaking, and to have Chester saying, 'Is she going in the fire now?' was very real.

I think a really valuable lesson is that as much as it might be painful to you or the kids to tell the truth, the truth will always out in the end, and if it isn't told at the beginning there'll be a lack of trust in the future.

Start scaring yourself

When the show *Life at the Extreme* asked me to present, I thought they'd got the wrong person. I am so risk-averse. I said to them, 'I don't want to be gutsy, gung-ho Davina. I just want to be stay-at-home-mum, cooking-nice-food Davina.' I suggested they ask my husband Matthew to do it. There were going to be four filming trips, away from my family for at least a week each time, to the most extreme parts of the earth, and I was just convinced I couldn't do it.

But *everybody* was telling me that it was a once-in-a-lifetime opportunity so, in the end, I agreed. Then I got cold feet and tried to pull out about six weeks before filming, but they told me I was really dropping them in it so I agreed to do just the first one in Namibia while they found other people to do the rest.

The thing I was *most* dreading was that there was going be a night out under the stars. I'm not a natural camper and I had to make my own boma – a wall of thorns to protect us from wild animals, from predators. I was making this boma, looking at this wall of thorns and thinking, 'Really? Is that going to stop a lion? Seriously?' There wasn't even a tent, just a fire. I was under the stars in a sleeping bag with a scarf over my head because it was absolutely freezing. And gradually I began to realise that it was exciting. Not just exciting, TOTALLY THRILLING!!! Normally, given a choice between a beach holiday or camping in Namibia, I'd have chosen the beach holiday. After doing this show, I've changed my tune. During that night, a lion came really close to the camp. I woke up to a commotion and people making noises. The ranger had his gun pointing straight at it. It sloped off, thank God. My time to keep guard was between one and two in the morning, half an hour after we'd seen the lion, and I have never been so awake in my entire life. I was looking for the two glinting eyes with the beam of my torch. So terrified. But next morning, as I was trying to warm my toes by the fire, I realised that when I got home, *that's* what I would talk to my kids about, camping out, having my close encounter with a massive predator, and what an incredible experience it was.

> **It was completely out of my comfort zone and it scared the bejesus out of me, but I loved it and will never forget it.**

So I ended up doing all the programmes. For 'Rainforest', I got stuck forty metres up a tree in Costa Rica in a thunderstorm and they had to do an emergency evacuation. Then there was my close encounter with a sperm whale. I nearly cacked my pants. It just swam straight towards me and I actually touched its back. And going in a submarine to 1,000 metres under the sea. And sleeping in a hut in the Arctic and going out for a wee in the middle of the night with a gun, pepper spray and a bear trap. FULL ON!

So, I've scared myself a lot with that show, but the added bonus I hadn't expected is that:

> **Something happens to your self-esteem and self-confidence when you set yourself a scary task _and get through it_.**

It is really magical. I think something like the Duke of Edinburgh Award is an amazing way of testing yourself within safe limits, where you can overcome a hurdle on your own or as part of a team, and you just feel good about yourself. I think scaring yourself or taking yourself out of your comfort zone is an absolutely genius thing to do – take it from me! I'm now an aficionado.

If they're mean, block them

I have lots of positive feedback on social media, and generally people follow me because they like me, but sometimes people follow me because I really annoy them. Some people are just trolls. There was a programme about trolls recently in which a troll admitted that their victim was nice but that he just wanted to rile them up. That's all they wanted . . . a reaction.

When Twitter first started I would see all the nice comments and not answer back much but would reply to every mean person. What's that about? After about six months I realised there was no point replying to people who are mean – they don't deserve it – so now I simply block them. I'm not talking about people who say, 'I normally like you, Davina, but I hated what you were wearing tonight,' or suchlike. I can take that, although it does hurt sometimes. I'm talking about people who say, 'You're a junkie scaghead.' The lesson I've learned is don't let them get under your skin. NEVER RESPOND. It only adds fuel to the fire.

Block them immediately. It gives you back your power.

I have had times when people were trolling me that I've actually felt frightened. I had some very real threats once on Twitter and the police got involved. It scared me, and now I just block them. What really did help me was to understand how trolls think. They troll because they think it's funny. They're not jealous, they don't hate you, and they're not trying to hurt you. It's hardly even personal. They genuinely think it's funny. They have no empathy so they just do it without being able to understand that it might hurt someone.

Reply to the good stuff and forget the bad. What's interesting is that in life (I don't know why) the bad comments often seem louder and bigger than the good. Out of two thousand comments, it's the three bad ones you remember.

I do have a couple of other techniques that help me. My children tease me mercilessly by repeating the little mantras I try to teach them in an American accent, and I'm like, 'Guys! You are taking the mickey but these are GOLDEN NUGGETS!'

'When somebody's angry *at* you but they're not angry *with* you, then put up the umbrella and their anger will rain over it but it won't touch you'. The other one is: 'If someone's being mean, put on your golden cloak. Put your hood up and don't let the negativity in!' In the past, if I've felt down and insecure, I'd put on this imaginary golden cloak (like the woman in the Scottish Widows advert) and feel like nothing could get to me. It's a metaphorical way of protecting myself, but the children think it's hilarious!

I'm forty-eight years old and I have to work at handling the negative stuff that comes my way. But if that sort of thing was happening to me when I was fifteen or sixteen then the best piece of advice I would give my teenage self is 'Don't go through it alone.' If you're too embarrassed to talk to a friend, or maybe you don't trust anybody, then call Childline – 0800 1111. Talk to somebody, anybody, it doesn't matter, but don't keep it to yourself because it becomes an enormous dark weight that you're carrying around and no one needs to feel like that.

Share it and the weight gets lighter.

Sometimes a self-esteem collapse happens despite your best efforts to keep the negativity of others away. You fall into a really dark hole and it's difficult to get yourself out again. If you feel like you want to stay in bed all day, under the duvet, and you don't want to do all the normal things like phone your mates or go to the pub, please go and see the doctor and talk it through, because depression is really serious. It's not necessarily something you're going to have for the rest of your life, it may be a brief moment and you just need a helping hand to get yourself out of a funk, but please don't suffer alone with it.

I have felt like I've been on the verge of depression a couple of times. Once was when I was pregnant with Chester and the whole *Davina* chat show debacle happened (read on to find out more about that), I felt like I was down a massive well looking up at life but I couldn't get up there. I was very hormonal and very upset, but I was lucky because Matthew didn't let me stay down the hole. He did all sorts of things that helped me recover, but if I hadn't had Matthew I hope I would have found someone to talk to about how I felt. I'll say it a LOT in this book . . .

Don't struggle alone.

Above: Me at two years old. With a muddy hand.

Left: My dad.

Below: My mum.

Below from right to left: My grand-father Pierrc (Pasha), my grandmother Olga (Masha), my dad Andrew, my mum Flo and my sister Caroline. The epitome of Frenchness.

Right: Me and Pippy. I'm two. Look at the way she's looking at me . . .

Left: My mum and my sister Caroline. Check out the boots.

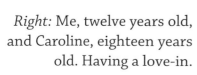

Right: Me, twelve years old, and Caroline, eighteen years old. Having a love-in.

Right: Buzz cut,
aged sixteen.

Below:
Me at twenty-two.

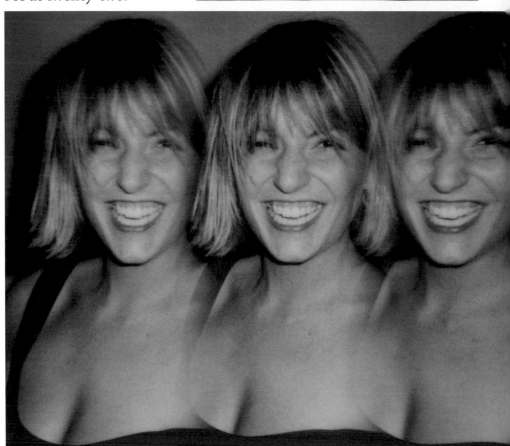

Above: Awesome wig. Me/Jessica Rabbit aged twenty-three.

Above: Working for MTV in Venice. I spent three years waiting to hold a mic with an MTV mic cube.

Dogs really are man's best friend

Right: Me and Rosie. I have Rosie to thank for everything. She found me Matthew.

Above: A selfie before people did selfies. I didn't get the smile memo.
Me and Matthew in Mauritius.

Above: Me and Pippy. Two peas in a pod.

Style it out

Styling it out is when something really embarrassing happens but you turn it to your advantage, usually by making a joke. I did it the other day outside Channel 4. It's a big building with a big reception and I was walking up the steps and I tripped and nearly fell over. My agent who was next to me went, 'Oh my God!' but I jumped up and went, 'Ta-dah!' So I got to my meeting and the guys there said, 'We saw you trip. Hilarious rescue!'

So style it out, it's much, much better, and to prove it, I'll tell you about my most embarrassing moment ever.

I was doing a show on Radio 2, covering for somebody, and I was invited to present an award at the Brits, the Radio 2 listeners award. I've hosted the Brits a couple of times and it's the best event ever. It's enormous, about six thousand people attend, and everybody gets horrendously drunk and misbehaves. It's *the* musical event on the British calendar, with amazing bands collaborating and performing together. It's just uber, uber, uber cool, so I was like, 'Yes, yes, yes, yes!'

There were about three months to go till the event so I went to see my friend Neil Cunningham, a designer and couturier, and asked him to make me something. He offered to do it for free since I was presenting an award so the outfit would be on the telly and the red carpet, which was so lovely of him, and he made this sexy secretary dress which made me feel totes amazing! I went down the red carpet and stopped to talk to all the press people. I did about ten quick interviews.

'Is it nice not to be working at an event?' some of them asked me.

'I *am* working. I'm presenting the Radio 2 listeners award,' I said, and on I went, doing more interviews and telling more people about the amazing award I was presenting. Finally, I got to my table where I was sitting next to the head of Radio 2. We chatted, she was lovely, and the lights dimmed.

'That's strange,' I thought. 'I wonder when I'm meant to go and present the award.' In the end, there was nothing for it but to ask. I was really worried they had forgotten to come and get me.

'When is the Radio 2 award being presented?' I asked her.

'It's first,' she said, and I was stunned. I should have been backstage getting ready. I got that sinking feeling. I could hardly get the words out of my mouth.

'Who's presenting it?' I asked.

'Robbie Williams, David Walliams and Matt Lucas,' she said, looking really pleased.

'Oh,' I said, but I was thinking, 'ARRGHGHGHGH!' I texted my agent under the table: 'OMG, I'm not presenting the award and I've just done the whole red carpet telling everybody that I am!' Then I heard the beep-beep beep-beep of the head of Radio 2's phone going with a message. She looked at her phone and clapped her hand over her mouth in horror.

'Oh my God, I am so sorry!' she said. Radio 2 had completely forgotten that they'd already asked me. I had to style it out. I had to laugh. I had to make a big joke of having done the red carpet and told everybody that I was presenting the award. Of course, part of me was dying inside and was so ashamed because Neil had made me the dress that would have cost a fortune, but there was nothing I could do. It was painfully embarrassing sitting through the whole dinner feeling that I'd been 'better-offered' but did it have a lasting effect on my career? Has anybody cared about it? No. Sometimes you've just got to style it out. I've been doing it a long time, it works . . . Trust me, I'm a presenter. Once, while I was still drinking, I stopped for a wee between two parked cars and told my friends I'd catch them up. It was about ten o'clock at night. It was dark. And mid-wee one of the cars turned their lights on. And I just turned round and waved at the people in the car, because what could I do? Got to style it out!

Mistakes are OK, but don't make the same one twice!

I did a chat show called *Davina*, and although I don't read much press, I knew something was going badly wrong because I was being hugged by members of the public in the aisles of the supermarket who felt bad for me. I was twelve weeks pregnant with Chester, quite hormonal and it was painful that that was my moment for a monumental TV turkey.

Matthew was amazing and jumped into hero mode. He wrote up a list of brilliant things in our life and stuck it on my computer: 'We have a brilliant life, we have a brilliant marriage, we have brilliant kids, we have brilliant pets, you have a brilliant career . . . You are brilliant, love, your husband.' At the bottom he wrote:

> **'To try and fail is temporary but not to try at all lasts for ever.'**

That expression really rang true to me.

It's awful, this idea that making mistakes or something going wrong is embarrassing or shameful. **Mistakes are brilliant!** They're the best tool ever. I learned a lot from doing that chat show.

The show had been called *Midweek McCall*, which to me sounded kind of groovy and had a bit of gravitas. We recorded the pilot on a set that had an industrial, warehouse feel. It was edgy and I was comfortable in it.

'This is the best pilot I've ever seen,' the head of the BBC said. 'This is absolutely fantastic. I love it.'

Because he liked it so much, they decided to make it more prime-time. I was already invested at that point, and that's when I felt like I'd lost my voice – because I felt like I should be so grateful for this big break.

'This is your job for the next ten years!' my agent at the time kept telling me. 'This is your *Graham Norton*. This is your *Jonathan Ross*. You'll be doing this for ever. This is amazing!'

'We'd just like to change the set a little bit,' the BBC said.

'Oh, but I like the industrial feel,' I replied.

'Well, no, everybody else here thinks that it would be much

better with a staircase and lights ... and we want to call it *Davina*.'

'Oh no, I think *Midweek McCall* is *much* better,' I said.

'*Davina* is great!'

I said I didn't want to call it *Davina*, again and again, but it got called *Davina* anyway.

'Well, they must know what they're talking about, they were the production team for *Parkinson*,' I thought. I had immense respect for them and felt like I should listen to what they said.

They changed the set to purples and pinks, put me in dresses and high heels when I had been in jeans and a T-shirt, and put in a big sweeping staircase that I had to walk down, with my name in enormous letters filled with lightbulbs! I was *so* embarrassed. It's not me and the public must have looked at it and thought, 'What the hell is this?'

Davina may have ended up as a TV turkey, but I learned SO much from it.

I learned that I can be a little bit star-struck around famous people, so actually doing a chat show with lots of famous people was not the best idea for me.

I learned not to use cards or an earpiece when I'm interviewing, because it stops you hearing what people are saying. I just want to talk to someone and listen to what they say. I probably would have been a lot better with the celebrities if I'd done that.

Most importantly, if someone wants me to do something I'm not comfortable with I've learned to say, 'I don't think it's me,' or 'I'm not doing that,' without feeling embarrassed. I no longer think I'm being 'difficult' by asking for what I want or need, which is a fantastic lesson to have learned. Being true to yourself and doing something that is genuine is where you're going to do the best work, because it's real. I think people can really see through stuff when you're not feeling comfortable.

I learned not to lose myself in what other people expected of me.

That lesson is one I've been learning progressively, bit by bit through my life, but *Davina* steepened the learning curve!

Afterwards, I went back to *Big Brother* and everybody forgot about my disastrous chat show ... Well, nobody forgot about it, but it was just a mistake. I think we need to applaud our mistakes as long as we learn from them.

Trust your instincts

When I read *Blink* by Malcolm Gladwell, I felt quite sad because it made me realise that I wasn't psychic. For many years I thought I was. *Blink* made me see that I was listening to my subconscious, my instincts.

When I lived in Paddenswick Road, in west London, something happened to me that made me think that I was psychic. I left my flat and shut the door but I didn't double lock it. As I walked to my car I got the willies, and even though it was quite a schlep, I went back and double locked the front door. When I came back later, all the other flats had been burgled but mine hadn't.

'Oh my God, I'm psychic!' I thought. 'I knew that was going to happen.' But *Blink* has taught me that, more likely, on the way to the car I saw something that my subconscious read as not being quite right which made me want to go back and lock the door. I wasn't lazy so I didn't think, 'Oh God, but it's all the way back there.' I listened to my instinct and I went back and it was very lucky I did!

In my work, interestingly, my instinct has generally been right. When I was offered that chat show by the BBC, I wasn't ecstatic. I just knew. I should have listened to my instinct. Now, my new agents always ask me, 'What do *you* think? What's your instinct telling you?' Trusting your instinct is about hearing your subconscious. I have learned to listen to my subconscious, my instinct, a lot more. If something or someone makes you feel a little bit uncomfortable, take note. We crush our instincts all the time but we should listen to them.

Be brilliant

Matthew met a man called Michael Heppell at a dinner party and was so impressed with him that he went out and bought his book *How to Be Brilliant*. Michael is a motivational genius; he writes books, gives speeches and coaches individuals and companies on how to change their lives for the better. I read the book and thought it was so good I ended up talking about him in a *Guardian* interview. He must have seen it because he got in touch and offered an hour and a half of his time as a way of thanking me. I said, 'Thanks, but I don't need it! I'm fine. I'm in a happy place,' but he was insistent so in the end I agreed. Right up until the day he was due to come I was going to cancel, but I felt bad so I went ahead. Now you can see that I don't always manage to say no when I want to! (Lols) In this case, I'm glad I didn't because it was the best, most life-changing hour and a half of my life.

When Michael arrived, he asked me what I wanted – not just with my career, but with my life, with everything! At that point, *Big Brother* was due to finish the following year and I was pretty sure nobody would want me after that and I'd have stopped working by fifty. He said, 'What would you *like* to happen?' I realised that I wanted to carry on working, and then I got a bit emotional because I suddenly understood that I'd reached so many of my goals that I didn't really have any left, I didn't know what I was doing. Where was I going? What was my focus? I thought, 'Oh God, I've only been talking to you for twenty minutes and I'm crying.'

I can honestly say that Michael Heppell took me off the train track that I was on and set me on a different path. It was a pivotal moment in my life. I totally changed direction and now I feel so positive and excited about my future. My career, which I thought was going to end the following year, is more fulfilling and exciting than ever! That was from an hour and a half with somebody I didn't think I wanted to spend any time with.

What I learned from Michael Heppell was to 'feel the fear and do it anyway'. He made me list three people I really admire and call them up to ask for a meeting about my future and any advice that they might be able to give me.

'Nobody's going to want to meet me!'

'Who do you want to meet?' he said.

'Simon Fuller,' I said. Simon Fuller started up 19 Management and he's an amazing businessman. He's the man behind brand Beckham, *American Idol* and *Pop Idol* and I didn't know him at all.

'Call him up now,' said Michael.

'What?! Now?! I can't call him up now, I haven't got his number.'

'You know what his company's called. Call his company.'

'I can't call his company.'

'Yeah, you can. Do it now. Let's do it now.'

'Oh my God, oh my God.' I got this huge surge of excitement, like I hadn't felt in ages. So I called up 19 Management and asked to speak to Simon Fuller. I was crossing my legs it was so embarrassing. He was away, so I left my number and put the phone down. Even without having spoken to him, I was running round the kitchen jumping up and down, screaming. It felt so brave just to call him out of the blue. It was not the kind of thing that I do. I wait for people to come to me. I was embarrassed to ask.

While we sat there, I got a call back from THE ACTUAL

Simon Fuller from America! His secretary had passed on the message and HE CALLED ME BACK! I didn't know what to say. In the end I managed to blurt out that I'd really love to meet him to bounce some ideas around and *he agreed*! I'm looking at Michael mouthing, 'Oh my God! He said yes!'

I put the phone down and I was crying tears of joy and thinking, 'This is insane!' The excitement I got by making ONE phone call was so much fun. Even if he'd never called me back I would have laughed about the excitement I felt that day. My heart was aflutter.

I think what Michael Heppell did was make me realise that I was in a bit of a rut. He made me understand that by taking myself completely out of my comfort zone I could change direction and that I had the power to do that. I didn't have to just sit by and let life happen to me. I think I had come to believe that I had lost that power. He completely changed the way I feel about myself. He empowered me to think the way I used to in my twenties. 'I want that. I'm gonna go get it.' Check out his books . . . they are BRILLIANT!

Four top tips if you don't have Michael on tap:

1. Michael gave me an amazing visualisation technique for fear.

    'When you think of fear, what colour is it?' he asked.
    'Red.' Whatever yours is, think of that.
    'What would calm be?' he said.
    'Blue.'

He taught me that when I feel fear welling up inside me to visualise catching it, stopping it, changing its colour from red to blue, and then pushing it back down again. I learned to do it with my hands as I was visualising, windmilling them up and then down.

It was quite funny. I remember once I was standing at the side of the stage at the BAFTAs, which are really scary because you look out into the audience and there are Ant and Dec and other celebrities that you love and have been watching on telly for ages, as well as every single boss that you've ever had or will have in TV, every producer, every TV star. It's absolutely terrifying going out onto that stage and I was standing at the side, doing waterwheel signs with my hands, one way and then the other, wondering if everybody was thinking I was doing some weird sort of dance. It does work though. It calmed my nerves and made me laugh.

2. 'How are you doing?' I ask my friend.

'I'm doing absolutely average,' he always replies.

It really depresses me! In *How to Be Brilliant*, the absolute number-one rule is when asked how you are, reply, 'I'm brilliant!', or 'great' or 'fantastic'.

Brilliant is a great word because it effervesces and shines. Try it when you're at work, if someone asks you how you are, say, 'I'm brilliant, thank you. How are you?' and watch their face light up.

Just don't say, 'I'm average.' Average is grey.

3. Michael Heppell suggested I buy a notebook and write down my goals in a very particular way. So, if you think, 'I want to be working for MTV by the time I'm 24,' write down: 'I'm Davina McCall and I'm working for MTV,' and put the date you want it to happen. You don't write 'I'm going to be doing this,' you write 'I'm a presenter on MTV.' Then you draw a little picture of yourself, a stickperson, but my stickperson would have a microphone with the MTV cube on (I used to see myself so clearly presenting with an MTV cube). Then you look at it every night, until you've got it in your head.

I didn't do this when I was younger, because I naturally thought in that way, but if you struggle with visualising something or you struggle with being able to retain a goal, write it down as if it is already happening, because when you have something set in stone you start actually doing things subconsciously to get you there. Your brain thinks, 'I'm going to be doing this so I'd better start putting things into place to make it happen.' It's very weird the way that it works, but it does. If you want to marry someone really kind you write: 'I'm married to a kind man/woman ...' It didn't work for me and George Clooney, but it does usually.

You can have loads of goals in your book. Fill it up and look at it every night. And in the back you can write your gratitude list of three things to be grateful for every morning. I have a little book by the bed with a pen always.

4. In the book, Michael has these great diagrams of wheels, each spoke being an important part of your life ... work, love, family, health, etc. Every few months you make a mark on the spokes according to how well you feel each area of your life is going and you can quickly see which parts of your life need a bit of maintenance (or a complete overhaul). It's really helpful because the results are often a surprise. Taking an overview like that is something we often forget to do. It stops you getting stuck in a rut.

Reframing

Do you say 'Every silver lining has a cloud' or 'Every cloud has a silver lining'?

I have a really vivid memory of a night, before I got into television and I didn't have much money, when I was out clubbing and had just enough to get a cab home, about seven quid. When I went to get my coat at the end of the night, my wallet had been nicked. I was really upset. Really, really upset because I didn't know how I was going to get home. I managed to beg enough money off someone to get the night bus, but I was still really upset. On the bus I thought to myself, 'You know what, maybe whoever took my wallet really needed it. Maybe the money in there will make a difference to them. It was only seven quid and it's going to be okay. I was only going to use it on a taxi and I'm on a bus and I'm still going to get home.' I talked myself around rather than sit in that toxic greyness of negativity. It wasn't instant and I had to do it verbally, because I was genuinely upset, but you can do that. It really works.

'I've got a magic wand and it's going to make you a positive person!' I wish I could say that! But I do honestly believe that with practice you can become more positive, and reframing negative situations so you see them with a different set of eyes is a brilliant place to start.

Smile more!

The TV programme I did with Rowland Rivron was called *Good Stuff*, and it was about what was happening in and around London. Rowland was *very* funny. He was so quick and witty, and I didn't really know what my place was in our duo. The producer of the show gave me a great tip. He said, 'Just let him be funny, he's a comedian, and don't try and be as funny as him because you're not.' He didn't actually say it quite that brutally although I did walk away a little bit like, 'Oh ...' Actually, that advice did make us a better presenting duo because I thought, 'Okay, this is me, I can stop trying to be something I'm not.'

Even so, I'd watch Rowland interview people and what was really clever about him (and something I used in all of my *Big Brother* interviews) was that he could ask really personal, toe-curling questions about a celebrity's private life, but because he did it with a really big smile or a laugh, it would take the heat out of the question. I also noticed that I just wanted to be near him all the time. I loved working with Rowland. He was quite possibly the funniest man I've ever, ever worked with, but he was also just really nice, lovely energy, fun to be around – though he never stayed around for very long!! If we took our eyes off him for one second on that show he'd be in the pub, lols.

I thought, 'What is it? What is it that makes you so funny? What makes me want to be around you all the time?' And I realised: 'You smile all the time.' I thought, 'I'm gonna smile more.' I did; it felt so nice *and* it had a really positive impact on me and on people that I was talking to. So Rowland Rivron taught me that. Thanks, Rowland!

Grit is a state of mind

I've only taken one day off work since I've been in TV.

When I was using and clubbing, I took loads and loads of days off work because I'd be extremely hung-over or still out of it and I just couldn't function. When I got clean, I found a new self-respect and it became really important to me that I stopped being so bloody selfish and self-centred.

As children, we are self-centred, as we should be, and as young adults we're still quite self-centred, but are beginning to wean ourselves off that as we enter a workplace and have to consider other people, or as we start a relationship. Then we have children and that's the ultimate selfless act because suddenly we have to look after somebody else's needs.

I think getting clean made me realise that I wasn't the centre of the universe and that other people depended on me. I suddenly understood that when I took a day off work it meant that my colleagues had to work extra hard or that the new models at Models 1 were extra nervous because I was the only person they knew and I was loafing around at home in bed. I realised that people needed me. It was like an awakening. After getting clean, a lot of my self-esteem came from the fact that I do matter. If I don't turn up it does count. I used to think that nobody cared if I didn't show up but they *do*, and that's stayed with me. Grit is a state of mind. The more I practise it, the more of it I have.

Nowadays, if I didn't turn up to an episode of *Long Lost Family*, for example, I'd be letting down people who have been waiting for years, sometimes for their whole lives, for news about their relatives. Me not turning up means rescheduling filming when they've taken days off work and letting the crew and the producers down. It would be bad, really, really bad, and so I work very, very, *very* hard not to do that, not to let people down. And because of that, I feel good about myself.

Taking lots of days off work on a sicky (or a jolly) allows you to relax, but in the long run you feel awful about yourself because you're just slacking. I don't want to feel like that about myself ever again. I've wasted a lot of time doing that. I want to do things that make me feel amazing, that make me feel like a good person. So if I feel ill and I'm meant to be working, I dose myself up with ginger or vitamin C or whatever will help, and get on with it.

Pippy was like that. I definitely get my work ethic from her. She never sat down. She was always on the go and worked tirelessly. My dad also wanted me to do something great, though he didn't tell me what it should be.

'I don't care if you don't go to university,' my dad always said, 'but whatever you do, give it everything you've got.' That was always his line and I was really grateful for it because almost all of my friends went to university and I didn't.

'It's all right if you don't go to university,' he said, 'but if you don't, get a job and be self-sufficient.'

They moved out of their house and into a flat when I was nineteen, so there wasn't any room for me. If I wasn't going to go to university, that was it. I had to stand on my own two feet. It was brilliant. That helped me get my grit.

Coping with criticism

A.A. Gill gave me a really great lesson once. We were at a party together and I was talking about a bad review I'd received. He looked at me and said,

'Davina, you can let it ruin your evening but don't let it ruin your breakfast.'

I think that's really good advice! So if I'm with somebody and they're having a moment about something not too serious, I say, 'All right, you can you let it ruin your breakfast but don't let it ruin your lunch.' Criticism is rarely worth ruining your day for anyway.

While I was doing *Big Brother*, I learned something really helpful about dealing with the negative judgements of others. People would go into that house, really nice people, but living in those conditions meant that sometimes you revealed your worst bits, which we all have, and when they came out they had to survive the crowd outside booing and shouting, 'We hate you!' I noticed that as soon as the evicted person walked close to the audience, they would stop shouting 'We hate you!' and call out, 'Hi! hi! We're over here! We love you!' It made me realise that disliking somebody, especially a celebrity, is pantomime.

At the beginning of my career I had to cope with a great deal of criticism because people were polarised by my enthusiastic behaviour. I am like an excitable puppy and some people find that annoying and other people love it. In life, not everybody's going to like you, but when you're famous people get to tell you that they don't like you.

Most of the time I don't put myself in a position where I see comments about myself. I don't read papers, I read *The Week* magazine (I'm never in that). I try to never read my own interviews because stuff gets slightly changed or interpreted in a certain way that might not be how I meant it, and then I find it hugely frustrating that I can't right that wrong, so I try not to read anything that's written about me, good or bad.

I have developed a slightly thicker skin and I've come up with strategies that are very similar to the ones I advise the kids: don't read it, don't let it ruin your day, move on and inter-act with nice people not nasty ones. Then the nasty people see that you never interact with them and they leave you alone.

Never moan about being famous

One of the lessons that I've learned in life is to never moan about being famous. If I hear somebody saying, 'It's really tough being famous because . . .' I'm like, 'STOP! You live in a lovely house, you get invited to things all the time, just shush now!'

Being famous has its downsides, in the same way that not being famous has its downsides, but I would never moan about it. What I *would* say is be careful *when* you get famous. I'm very, very grateful that I got famous after I got clean and after I was twenty-five, which meant that I'd worked in the real world and I'd struggled to pay my rent and so I was really grate-ful for everything that was happening. It also meant that I was slightly more robust to deal with the press than I would have been at eighteen.

The only time I think fame and success is NOT a good thing is when you're young. I know that a lot of kids are following vloggers and they want to get themselves out there on the internet, on YouTube – I really understand that. My kids want that too. But dealing with fame and the trolls that come with it at thirteen, fourteen, fifteen, when you are quite vulnerable and you're still learning how to deal with emotions, is tough.

It's hard enough just dealing with people at school, let alone the entire nation.

I always say to my kids, 'I'm so proud of you, I want to show you off, to show everybody how beautiful and brilliant you are, but when you're throwing up outside a party because you've had too much to drink on the one mistaken binge that you have, do you want the paparazzi up your nostrils? I've kept you out of the public eye so that you are allowed to make those mistakes in private. But, by God, when you're ready and when I'm ready, I'll be taking you everywhere!' I'd love to do fun runs with them and stuff for charity, but at the moment I can't because I truly believe that fame at a young age is not a good thing. Trust me on this!

I have never met a grown person who became famous when they were a teenager who doesn't feel like it massively messed them up.

So, I never moan about fame, but I do treat it with caution. Like many things in life, too much too young, can have bad results.

4

How to Stay Married

Dreaming

I didn't really understand what visualisation was when I was younger but now I realise it's what I've always done. I've been such a dreamer all my life. My dream of happiness is always in my head.

When I was younger, my dream featured me wearing an apron over a pretty, flowery, Cath Kidston-style dress, wellies, my hair in a ponytail with a fringe – like my hair is now – sort of messy, looking out over the countryside, married with two or three children running round the kitchen, a bit chaotic. Because I had such a strong picture in my head of where I wanted to go, I think I made that happen. Interestingly, people always think that I must have known where I wanted to go with my work but work's been something that's just progressed and led me to my dream: the house in the country, the pinny, the animals and the children and the chaos and the husband. That was my dream, a lot more than work was.

If you can picture something in your head, not of where you want to go but of where you *will* be, you can just make it happen. It's an amazing tool.

How to have fireworks when you kiss

I first met Matthew when I was walking my dog in the park. As usual, I was wearing ultra-casual clothes, dungarees, a vest and a pair of welly-bobs, and no make-up. I was with my wonderful, faithful dog Rosie, from Battersea Dogs Home, when round the corner came this beautiful boxer dog and following the dog was a man with a cap on . . . and he was hot. I said, 'Hello!' and he looked at me a bit quizzically, and said, 'Hello.'

I carried on walking, thinking to myself, 'Oh God, he looked at me like I was a complete fruit loop. Damn it! Oh well, maybe I'll bump into him again if I'm meant to. What am I gonna say to him? How am I gonna get talking to him?' So I kept walking, thinking, 'Please bump into him, please bump into him.'

And I did! He was in the area where you're allowed to let your dogs off the lead and I went in and said, 'Hey! Sorry I said hi earlier. I thought you were somebody that I'd met yesterday. Are you new here? I know everybody normally. This is my area.'

'I am quite new, we just moved back.' He said 'we' and I was like, 'Ah. End of.' You know, leave it, leave it!

'We moved back from New York quite recently.'

'What, you and your girlfriend?'

'Yes, but we've split up.' I was thinking, 'Uh-uh, no. Back away. Radioactive.'

'How long were you together?'

'Five years.' Clearly on the rebound. In grief, really bad.

'Oh no, I'm so sorry.'

'No, don't be. It's fine.' He sounded like it really was, so we carried on talking about dogs and laughed a lot. Then I walked away, sure we would bump into each other again. When Matthew tells this story he just says, 'Yeah, I met her in the park and I thought she was lovely,' and that's it, but I remember every single minute of it.

When we bumped into each other again I suggested walking our dogs together. People I used to see in the park started asking me why I was suddenly wearing flowery dresses, like someone in *The Postman Always Rings Twice*, with my wellies – they could tell something was up! We just walked and walked and walked our dogs until eventually I was looking after his dog if he was working and he looked after mine if I was working.

At that time I was having counselling with this *amazing* woman called Suzy. She guided me through those eight weeks after I met Matthew.

'I think he's really nice,' I would tell her.

'Well, if you think he's really nice, he probably is really nice.'

'I always go for people I need to fix, but this time it feels different. I don't feel like I am.'

'Well, he probably isn't someone you need to fix then,' she would say. 'You're seeing him through a different set of eyes.'

It was true. I had become much more self-aware. Suzy also explained that it was a person's underlying values and aspirations that I needed to see if I could be happy with, rather than trying to fix them.

'What's really important in a relationship', Suzy explained, 'is whether you feel the same about vital issues like money, saving, housing; whether you want to live in London, the country or abroad; do you want kids; are you into disciplining your kids or are you very relaxed?'

I'm not saying I talked to Matthew about these when I first met him, but every time one of these topics came up and we agreed, I'd mentally go TICK!

After much walking, I invited Matthew round for tea and he got absolutely rinsed by my sister Caroline.

'How old are you? Where are you from? What are your parents like? How many brothers have you got? Are you close to your brothers? Do you love your mother?' she demanded, firing questions at him like the Gestapo.

'Wow, Caroline, that was a bit gruelling for Matthew,' I said afterwards.

'Well,' she said, with a wonderfully Gallic shrug of the shoulders, 'you 'ave a terrible track record wiz ze men zat you meet; but I like 'im.'

He passed the Caroline test with honours, and then, after eight weeks of walking and getting to know each other, I remember Matthew was sitting on my sofa and I went and sat on the coffee table opposite him at four o'clock in the afternoon, and we kissed. And we kissed for absolutely hours and then we took our dogs for their evening walk together. We got locked in the park because we were kissing under a tree. We had to lift the dogs over the fence and clamber over to get out!

The next day I went to work on a programme called *The Real Holiday Show* on Channel 4 and my chin was scabbing because I'd snogged so much. The make-up artist said, 'Well, I'm assuming that you've kissed him?' I was like, 'Yeah, there was a lot of pent-up sexual energy.'

Eight weeks between first meeting and first kiss. It was a record.

And the lesson I learned from that was that a snog tastes much better when you know someone really well. A casual snog in a club can be good fun but when you get to know them better you might think, 'What a doozy,' and wish you hadn't snogged them. Eight weeks is quite a long time, actually, by anybody's standards, but even just getting to know them a bit makes the first kiss much nicer. A conscious kiss: I have chosen to do this. It meant much more to both of us and that's why we got the fireworks.

Once Suzy could see that I was settled, that I'd worked through my obsession for bad boys, she said, 'I think you can stop seeing me now.' She was right . . . I never looked back.

*

Don't chuck people because they're wearing the wrong shoes

OK, so you're out on a date with a guy and he seems nice, you've had a really good evening, but you think his shoes are hideous, or the pattern on his shirt is so offensive that it makes you angry, or he's wearing a shark-tooth necklace and it makes you want to vomit.

These are all minutiae! They are not his personality.

He probably just wasn't sure what to wear and thought, 'This might look nice.' I mean, some guys couldn't give a hoot what they wear and just try to make a bit of an effort for you. Maybe they've never worn the shoes before but they thought, 'I'll crack these ones out, they're clean.'

To judge somebody on their outside is very easy to do and, OMG, I used to do it. But it's a sad thing to do, because often you're going to miss out on some really, really wonderful people. Let me tell you my own experience.

I'd been with Matthew for a week (snogging for a week; we'd been walking for nine weeks). I really liked him. He was a very nice guy, very grounded, very kind, thoughtful, funny and seemed to have an amazing family. I mean, he was ticking all the boxes, and so I invited him to my thirty-first birthday party. I hadn't quite taken into account how terrifying that would be for him. He had only just found out that I was quite famous and he was about to meet everybody I'd ever known, including my family, all at once.

Anyway, it was a free bar and he got really drunk because he was so nervous. I immediately thought, 'Oh no, he's an alcoholic! I knew there had to be something wrong with him.' During that party he did some of the most extraordinary dancing I've ever seen in my entire life, in the middle of the dance floor, sticking his tongue out, pointing fingers. I was like, 'Oh my God, I don't know if I can be with you.' I was really embarrassed (which says more about me at that time than it does about him, but I didn't know that then) and between the alcohol and the dancing, I decided to call it all off.

I met him the next morning in a café and he made me laugh *so* much that I thought, 'Oh sod it, he's hysterical. I love him. I don't mind about the dancing.' I *did* mention the alcohol.

'I've got to be quite careful because it's important to me that I'm not with somebody who's an alcoholic,' I said.

'Are you mad? I'm not an alcoholic!'

The upshot of this story is that his dancing is now one of *my most favourite things about him*. I love the fact that he totally releases when he gets a bit tipsy on the dance floor and goes absolutely mad. In fact, I actively encourage it because it's so great. He's so free and I admire that.

What I'm saying is, if you've met someone you really like but he's wearing the wrong shoes or he's wearing the wrong trousers, these are the superficial things that don't matter when you've been together for eighteen years. It's something that you might even come to love. My horror at his dancing was a lot more about me thinking I was really cool than it was about him. He's a great dancer. Everybody else thought he was a great dancer. Everybody else thought he was really fun. I just saw it as deeply, deeply embarrassing. But that's about me. And what he's taught me is that it's a really admirable thing to be free. So don't chuck people if they're wearing the wrong shoes (or dancing madly), but ask yourself, do you like them? Are they a good person? Do they make you laugh? Those are the things that REALLY matter.

You can't change people

One of the best lessons I ever learned is that you can't change somebody else. I must have heard that a thousand times in my twenties but I consistently went out with people who I tried to make into the person I wanted them to be. I would fall in love with somebody's potential, which is the most painful thing to do, and not only for you: it's awful for the other person too as they constantly feel they're never good enough.

I remember one boyfriend in particular, who was probably one of the smartest men I'd ever met, that I could just listen to for ever. I am always deeply impressed by great intellect, I guess because I didn't go to university. I'm brilliant in the school of life, but in the school of education I have a lot to learn. When I meet somebody with tons of information to teach me, I just love it. I was completely blown away by him and thought, 'My God, this guy is going to be so successful.'

'You're such a good writer. You'd be an amazing journalist!' I would say.

'I want to be a musician,' he would reply.

I had lots of ideas for him and would get quite annoyed when he didn't go along with them. I was frustrated because I just couldn't *hear* him. In fact, what my constant nagging did was push him further away from where I wanted him to be. He just wasn't going to conform, and certainly not to what I wanted him to do.

I look back now and realise that he must have felt that I didn't love him for who he was. I was trying to make him be something that he just didn't want to be.

He decided to be a bicycle courier. It's a perfectly fine job and he made good money, although it scared me rigid because I was sure he was going to get knocked off his bike any minute, but it was like he was kicking back at me. But his real passion, just as he'd said, was music. He became a brilliant guitarist. If I'd left him to his own devices, he would probably have come to that much quicker than he did with me trying to push a square peg into a round hole.

When people wouldn't change the way I thought they should I got so annoyed, when instead I should have been looking for somebody I loved just as they were. Sometimes it's quite tough if somebody's exceptionally hot and fit (I know that's very shallow) not to think, 'Goddammit, can't I just squeeze you into the person that I need you to be?' But sadly it doesn't work because you just end up really pissed off, and so do they.

It was SO good when I stopped that.

Now I'm married to Matthew and I've been with him for years and years and years and years and I know the man that I married and I knew who he was when I married him. Instead of trying to change him, I have learned to compromise. He might not agree with me of course. He'll probably come out with a book called *Lessons I've Learned*. And so he should. Anyway, marriage is about compromise and sometimes I feel that I make too many compromises, and I'm sure he does too; but I can't change Matthew, he can only change himself, and knowing that makes me less angry.

The four kinds of love

My dad taught me about the four kinds of love that you need in a marriage. Friendship, desire, respect and trust.

A relationship without friendship means you don't like each other, so that's the end; a relationship without desire just becomes a friendship, so that's not a relationship; a relationship without respect means that there is a complete and utter breakdown in all areas. If you don't respect each other then there is contempt. I read this amazing thing in *Blink* by Malcolm Gladwell, about a man who had trained himself to talk to couples. He said that within fifteen minutes he could tell with 95 per cent accuracy whether a couple were going to be together in fifteen years. After further years of training he got it down to about three minutes. The question he asked was: How did you meet? If he saw one tiny jot of contempt, eye-rolling, huffing, anything like that, it was the death knell.

Trust? Trust you can rebuild I think, but it takes a long time. Trust doesn't have to be about fidelity. It can be a lie. Trust is fragile and it's the one that only time will heal. I've used my dad's four kinds of love in every sexual relationship that I have had (if you are reading this, Matthew, or the kids, I've only had one . . .); if you don't have all four, friendship, desire, respect and trust, forget it.

Soulmates?

I don't think there is such a thing.

When I met Matthew, he wasn't at all the kind of guy who would normally give me a fire in my pants. The guys who did that were always the really bad boys, and there was nothing bad about Matthew. He was a very lovely guy. I got to know him a bit and we hung out and we kissed and it was really lovely. Really, really lovely. I thought, 'Oh God, *this is different*.'

When people talk about 'soulmates', I think they mean someone who thinks and feels the same as they do about everything, someone completely on the same wavelength, totally synergistic, 'we think the same, we agree on everything' kind of person.

I'm at a stage in my life where I and a lot of my friends have been with our husbands for fifteen to twenty years. Do any of us feel like that about the people we're married to? No. We share interests. We have fantastic fun at dinner parties, but we're all quite different from our spouses.

I think, as I get older, that this notion of a soulmate is quite misleading. I think it's more helpful to think, 'Is this somebody I'll be able to get through thick and thin with, share my life with?' For me, I wanted a man who would drag me into his cave, a man's man – well, my God, I got that, and love it! I wanted somebody who would be faithful and true to me and loyal to our family and I've got that. These are things that are really important to me and I would not swap them for the world.

I remember when Matthew and I got engaged, I was thinking, 'How can I know this is for ever? It's such a huge thing, getting married. How do I know? Is he my soulmate? What is that?' I worried I was allergic to his style of dancing, but eighteen years on I love his dancing – how would I have known that? The stuff we argue about usually has something to do with the kids, but how could I have known that before we had them? Marriage is a leap of faith in so many ways, but Matthew's core beliefs, his values and his goodness were a really great start. I think we come from the same page on that level.

That's what I've learned. More than any notion of being a 'soulmate', you need to make sure you have common values and can share some common interests. These are the things that keep you together, or bring you back together after a row.

Last night, I was tucking Tilly into bed and Matthew got in the other side and we all had a real laugh. After he went Tilly said, 'I loved that.' Those are the little things that I really cherish, especially if we've been through a bad patch or something's been tough and you have a moment like that and you think, 'God, it really is worth it.' It's worth holding on to.

Say less, mean more

I am such a culprit of overthinking everything. I have to remind myself to keep it simple. You don't have to overdo something or overthink something or overspeak something for it to be an incredibly powerful experience.

There's a great bit in John Gray's book *Men Are from Mars, Women Are from Venus* which says to men that if you are going to get flowers for a woman, one single flower will mean as much as a hundred. Guys often think that they need to make huge gestures, buy a whole florist shop of roses, but they don't.

Matthew came to pick me up from the airport when I got back from Costa Rica. It had been a really tough trip, I'd felt really sick on the plane, I think I had terrible flu and I had a hookworm in my leg. I was a real mess and very, very tired. I've never been so happy to see his face ever. It was a total surprise, I thought it was going to be a driver, but that simple gesture meant more to me than anything.

Here are some of the texts Matthew has sent me that I've kept because they meant so much to me. Generally they're ones that come out of the blue and they're very straightforward:

7 March, 09:33
I love you very much xx

12 June, 14:15
It's all good. Lots going on. Don't worry.
One day at a time.

I was on a shoot once and we were having a five-minute break. It was a *Long Lost Family* shoot and there's always a soundman, a cameraman, a camera assistant who also does second camera, a director and me. Generally speaking, camera and sound are usually men. During this break I got a text from Matthew and I said, 'Aw, Matthew's just sent me a text saying "I love you" for no reason. That's so nice.'

'Is that not a bit mushy?' all the guys said in unison.

'No, it's lovely. Girls love that kind of stuff. It's very re-assuring. It's even better when it comes for no reason, when it's not an "I love you, can I go to the pub?" or an "I love you, I want da-da-da." It's just for nothing,' I said. 'You send your other halves an "I love you" text and see what happens.' So they did, and all of them got really amazing responses!

I'm a really simple creature. Reassurance, an arm round me, a 'You're doing great, I love you.' Simple things said with honesty mean a lot. To my mind, they mean an awful lot more than elaborate, fluffed-up stuff, which somehow seems slightly insincere. A hundred roses is a bit showy-offy. It says more about *you* than it does about the gesture.

*

Random acts of kindness

There's a guy called Danny Wallace who I presented a show with many years ago. He's a comedian who became a cult leader when he started a movement called Join Me. He put an advert in *Loot* asking people to 'Join me' and send a passport-sized photo. It was totally on a whim, he had no idea what he wanted to do and hadn't expected much response, but thousands of people sent in their photo and wanted to know what they were joining! So Danny decided that the 'Joinees' would form a Karma Army and perform random acts of kindness (RAoK) on Fridays, henceforth known as Good Fridays. The RAoK was best if anonymous and, after a while, he decided that they could happen at any time, not just on Fridays. The 'collective' really took off and had about twelve thousand Joinees participating in this.

One time, Danny got all his cult followers to meet at Tottenham Court Road for a *Karmageddon*. They all brought a present with them worth ten pounds or less with a label on it saying 'From Join Me member in Japan' or Australia or wherever they came from, and at two o'clock on that Friday they all dispersed through the streets of London, giving out their presents to whoever walked past. Then they ran off! It was amazing! After that he wrote a book called *Join Me*, about the things he or his cult followers had done for other people.

It was really, really sweet and got me thinking about how

much fun random acts of kindness are. The easiest one that I do, and I do it every single time, is pay for the car behind me at a road toll, even if it's the Severn Bridge, which is quite expensive. If we're in America it's sometimes two bucks, but at Disney it's fifteen dollars to go through. Matthew did a really ace one the other day. He went to pick up some takeaway pizzas and he paid for every single pizza in the restaurant. He just picked up everybody's tab and then left, so nobody knew who'd done it.

There are quite funny ones where you drop a fiver on the floor near a granny and then pick it up and say to her, 'I think this dropped out of your bag...' It's selfish in a way, because it just makes you feel so goddamn good. It's got to be a random, preferably an *anonymous* act of kindness, because then there is only altruism.

Sometimes I do a RAoK that is not anonymous, like giving someone a lift. This is a risky tactic if you are a woman alone in a vehicle, so you have to pick the people that you're going to give a lift to quite carefully. I won't give a lift to any children, because obviously they're always being told not to get into strangers' cars, and I won't give a lift to a man, although I have given a lift to a man with a bicycle who had a puncture and no repair kit and I had the kids in the car. The kids all said to me, 'Mum, you are insane. You should not pick up that man,' but I didn't think he'd massacre all four of us. And he had a bicycle (and I'm a fellow cyclist) and was really in need.

Brenda is somebody I've been giving lifts to for a few years. I first met her on a really cold morning. She has this blaze of beautiful white hair, which makes her look really cute and granny-like. I drove past her at the bus stop and thought, 'Shall I? Shan't I? Shall I?' I reversed a bit and got out and asked if she wanted a lift anywhere. She only wanted to go the village before mine so I said, 'Absolutely, it's on the way. Jump in.' She had no idea who I was. It was only on the third time she got in my car, she asked me, 'Are you Davina McCall?'

'Yup.'

'Oh.' That was it. Whenever I see her I always give her a lift. She's lovely. Her granddaughter contacted me on Twitter and said, 'I think you give my granny a lift sometimes and we all just wanted to say thank you,' and that made my heart sing a bit.

Little kindnesses make a BIG difference

When you've been with somebody for a long time, sometimes the little niceties go. It's easy to think that if you're giving a birthday present to your other half it's got to be something big because you've been together for so long. Let me tell you . . . it doesn't. A small, thoughtful present means so much more. I'm not convinced by Valentine's Day for the same reason, because I think that we should be telling each other that we love each other and giving little heart-shaped chocolates (obviously sugar-free) every day, *not just on Valentine's Day*.

Matthew and I were unbelievably romantic in our first two years. I came home once and he had made a trail of rose petals and lychees (I'm obsessed with lychees) up to our bedroom. He came to surprise me in Manchester once; he just turned up while I was working there. That night, when I got back to the hotel room, he had put a 'Do not disturb' sign on the bedroom door. When I went into the bathroom and looked at the mirror, he'd written 'SO PROUD' in my lipstick. He'd put the 'Do not disturb' sign out so they didn't come in and clean it off the mirror. That was a long, long time ago but I'm still kind of dining out on that.

Now, eighteen years on, he turns on my electric blanket even if he's not having his on (I know ... Don't say anything about the electric blanket. I LOVE it!), or he'll run me a bath. It's those things that mean a lot in the end. I got a bench for him in honour of his dad and I know that meant a lot to him. I put Post-its in his suitcase when he goes away, or I'll make him a cup of coffee in the morning. Those little things matter and I've definitely been guilty of neglecting this when I think I haven't got enough time or I need him to do something for me. What happens is that you both end up shutting down and nobody's doing anything for anybody because both people think, 'Why should I do anything for you because you don't do anything for me?' Then you're in really big trouble because then you're locked down. So keep making those little gestures.

*

Escaping lockdown

If a relationship does enter lockdown, there are some great ways out of it.

One of my favourites is the egg timer trick. It's amazing. It's a way to talk to each other without the interruptions, the 'Yes, but you said . . .' Interruptions are very dangerous, they rapidly escalate any argument because:

1. Neither of you is feeling heard.
2. Both of you get defensive.
3. Walls go up.
4. Lockdown happens.

The best way I've found to avoid it is to sit down together when the kids are in bed, you're at home, not in a public place. You get an egg timer and you each take three minutes to say how you're feeling. The other person is not allowed to interrupt, to shout, to argue, to get up. They just have to sit and listen and try not to think only about what they're going to come back with! Then they get to reply in their three minutes. Then you carry on doing this, back and forth, for at least half an hour. Even if the person talking has run out of things to say but the egg timer's still going, the other person does not get an opportunity to speak. You have to sit in silence until the egg timer has finished, because that person might think of something else.

What's interesting about the egg timer trick is that you

take the time to really understand how the other person is feeling. So if Matthew said to me, 'I feel like you're not telling me enough about the kids' activities. You're not including me,' normally, I would reply, 'I haven't got time, I'm busy.' I'd defend myself. If he has a full three minutes to say it, he'll explain 'and it makes me feel like this . . .' and I'll feel a bit bad because I can suddenly see where he's coming from. Then, the best place to get to, which we do usually get to with the egg timer, is where we'll actually say, 'I'm sorry about that.' Mutual apology is amazing.

Half an hour is not long out of your life but if you do that once a month, it's a relationship top-up without needing to go to counselling. You can talk to each other without it escalating and, when you know you've got three uninterrupted minutes, you can broach some of the heavy stuff. I'm taking note BTW because we don't do this once a month . . . working on that!

Always try and talk about how you're feeling rather than accusing the other person of making you feel a certain way. Look at each other. It makes the person talking feel heard and seen and it will create an atmosphere of feeling sympathetic towards each other.

Another way to escape lockdown is to do the things you enjoyed when you were first together. Make time to do them without the kids. Sometimes, when you're on lockdown, you don't want to spend any time with that person at all. So even fifteen minutes is good. Matthew and I love a box-set. Even if we're not talking, just sitting next to each other sharing a box-set together is bonding.

When we're on lockdown, and we're back to back in bed, I'll just put a hand on Matthew – it's not a hug or a spoon, it's a connection.

'I'm still here. I do still care about you. We're ships passing in the night but I'm still here,' is what that is saying.

Probably three times out of five during a disagreement, Matthew and I start laughing.

'This is really stupid. Shall we just forget it?' we both say.

The new dynamic of modern relationships

I consider myself to be a strong, robust, opinionated woman. I am seeking equality in my workspace and at home and I think that it's hard for guys to keep up with how fast women are changing. In my grandmother's day, if you weren't married by twenty-one, you were on the shelf. When you got married, you became a housewife and looked after your husband and stayed with him for ever and that was that. By the sixties anyone could get divorced, there was free love and the Pill, but generally speaking, there was no equality in the workplace. By the eighties women were beginning to start getting some of the top jobs in business and politics, and now I think we're doing quite well, but often women who have jobs are still finding themselves doing the majority of the parenting, or organisational stuff to do with the parenting, like checking school kit, washing the kit, making sure it's labelled, sorting out birthday presents and all that.

So we are getting better at equality in the workplace, women are getting top jobs in companies (although we've still got a way to go with equal pay), and we've got an amazing support network because we have each other, we have fought hard to get a vote and have rights and be considered equal to our men, but at the same time we're the ones who give birth and we're the ones who take a year off and do the majority of the child rearing and we're the ones who are often expected to cook an evening meal and keep house, because it's the traditional thing ... but actually, something's gotta give. We can't physically or mentally do all of those things. I think equality in the home is just as important as in the workplace. I think a modern marriage has to be viewed as teamwork. If a woman is bringing home the bacon as well as the man, then the man needs to share half of the other chores. If we're earning half the crust but doing more than half of everything in the home, that's not equality. The modern dynamic has to be about finding the balance.

I was laughing the other day, thinking about the film *Magnolia* in which Tom Cruise says, 'Respect the cock.' He's giving a workshop about how you can have sex with the secretary at work, it's really *eugh*! But in a funny kind of way, we need to be vigilant that, while we're seeking equal rights as women, we don't emasculate men and defeminise ourselves. I want equal rights and I want to share chores in the house and share the burden of life together with my partner to feel like a team, but at the same time I don't want him to turn into a pushover. I want it to be equal and that's an unbelievably delicate balance.

Listening to successful women friends of mine, it seems hard for a guy to feel he's not the provider. If he's not, what is he? I think if a husband isn't the main provider he can still be a great husband, great dad, great man. It's not all about the man working and the woman being a housewife – it's not as clear as that any more. If I go out and earn money and you go out and earn money, we've got to share stuff. That is true equality. It's not 'What's for dinner?' It's 'Who's cooking tonight?'

I don't think men are bad. I just think that men and women need to come together and work as a team. I think things will get better for the next generation and it'll be even better the generation after that; but right now I think we're in a time of transition and a lot of us are struggling with finding our place. I mean, Matthew and I struggle with it all the time because I'm successful and not only that, I'm famous, and that's really hard. We've come up with strategies to help us, like not going to too many red-carpet events because, of course, it's devastating for him to be called 'Mr McCall' (that has ACTUALLY happened).

I read somewhere that people work brilliantly on a six-hour day and they get exactly the same amount achieved as they do in a ten-hour day. So why don't companies allow greater flexibility to their employees? That way, men could help more at home and women would be in much, much higher positions of power, as we'd be happier continuing to work if everybody could leave at 5 p.m. That would be a no-brainer. If you're reading this, CEOs: sit up and listen. Spread the word. We need to change this country's attitudes towards work and the workplace. For men and their connection to their children, what about longer paternity leave? That would be absolutely fantastic. It would change *everything*!

I've just had an amazing idea. I think we should start *DadsNet*.

Don't sweat the small stuff

I think this is a great saying. If you've been in a relationship for a long time then the small stuff, the little things that you once loved about somebody, can suddenly make you want to stab a pillow. They can drive you so mad that you want to scream into a cushion. I'm just trying to think if there's something that Matthew does ... I mean, there's a list (only joking, Matthew) – but let me think of one good example. Matthew insists on giving everybody a ridiculous nickname. It's a family trait. I'm Dickledax to his family. Everybody gets a big nickname. Normally nicknames are shorter than your name but his are always really, *really* long. Over the eighteen years I have had a succession of at least twenty different nicknames ... and they've all been horrific. In our honeymoon period, which normally lasts about eighteen months to two years, when your lover could literally fart or poo in your presence and you'd think it was lovely, he used to call me Puppy and I quite liked that. I thought that was sweet. It used to make everybody else want to throw up but I thought it was really cute. Then it turned into Falafel and he'd say it in a really silly voice. In a supermarket, anywhere, he would shout, 'Falafel!' It sounded like he had Tourette's because it's quite a weird word to shout in an aisle: you could see people wondering whether he had a thing about shouting the names of vegetarian foods. I'd reply and people would look over and say, 'Isn't that Davina McCall? Did he just call her Falafel?' It's embarrassing. There's been Schnaflank, which isn't even a word. Schniebel. Schnivel, which I *really* hated.

I like the name Davina. It's not as if I've grown up thinking I need to change my name to Scarlett. I *love* the name Davina. I like it when people call me Davina. I don't need a nickname. Over the years I've asked him to call me my name, sometimes in quite direct language. He just says, 'Sorry Schnivel.' He thinks that's really funny. And the angrier I get the funnier he thinks it is and the more he does it. Recently he was calling me Kilimanjaro. I don't understand why. I've never climbed Kilimanjaro. I'm not going to climb Kilimanjaro. Now it's just Kili. He called our poor nanny, whose name was Bobby-Jo, Spleen. *Spleen!* Why Spleen?

Anyway, you get my gist and can probably tell it winds me up . . . but . . . on a good day I ask myself, 'Is this worth getting yourself so riled up about that you want to divorce him?' No. It's not. That's compromise.

*

Voice disagreements

I have grown up in a matriarchal family. My mum, although she was tipsy a lot of the time, was a driving force, a feisty enigma, a no-nonsense feminist who gave as good as she got and was sexually liberated. It made her very attractive to just about everybody. My Spanish grandmother and her Portuguese maid, Maria, were very strong, as was my granny, Pippy. Her mum, Lulu, was an amazing businesswoman and my great-grandma, Mickey's mum was incredible too. My stepmum worked and there was equality at home. I was surrounded by really strong female role models so I've always felt that I should voice my opinion and that it matters. At home, when I was growing up, it was not bad to disagree with somebody and it didn't have to turn into a massive fight. My family was full of confrontational, opinionated people and that taught me that if somebody tells me I'm wrong, far from being frightened or threatened, I love it! That's mental fencing and I approach almost every kind of disagreement with an attitude of jousting.

I think voicing your disagreements in a relationship is really important. Sometimes Matthew and I walk away from each other and agree just to leave it if it's a small matter, something petty. Stupid stuff is sometimes fine to leave. But when it's a big issue, like the kids' welfare or their futures or something like that, we can't just walk away. Those are the arguments that come back six months later if we walk away and then become a massive barney. In those important matters, oh my God, I drive Matthew mad because I'll follow him round the house saying, 'I think we need to say it. I'm not done. I need to just say it.' Poor guy. But he does let me ... and we do talk ... and it helps. It's much better to talk things through, that way we can prevent a lot of pointless arguments in the future.

When I first met Matthew, if we had a disagreement and he walked off, I'd just keep following him round the house. Matthew would say, 'I'm going to give you five minutes to talk it through, but then we have to finish because it's not important.' So I'd get my five minutes and then I'd walk away.

So I have learned that there are times when I need to walk away and drop something. Not getting Matthew to see my point of view leaves me frustrated and antsy but if I keep going back it doesn't solve anything. In those instances, Matthew and I concede that we have different opinions and the heat of the moment is not the time to talk about it. We have learned to just walk away. If it is a big issue that needs re-addressing, we come back to it when we've taken the heat out of the argument ... It's usually about the kids or money, like pretty much every other couple, and we talk about it when we can do so without shouting. I'll say, 'Look, what I'm trying to say is that I understand where you're coming from, but what I meant was ...' because really, all we want to be is heard. 'I see your point of view. You see my point of view.' Sometimes you can do this better if you walk away from a heated argument and come back when you're calmer.

Something I've learned from recovery is that everything is

better when I talk about it from my experience rather than do Matthew's thinking for him. I try not to say, 'You do this, you think this,' because that might not be his experience (when I forget not to do this, it's always bad). He might not think or feel like that. If I say, '*I feel* like you're doing this,' I haven't said, '*You're* doing it,' I've only said what it feels like to me. So it's about my experience rather than pointing the finger. This is a very effective way to communicate because I'm not blaming. Matthew doesn't have to go on the defensive, and I actually have a chance to sort things out rather than escalating them.

Get involved

This is one I've only just learned myself. If Matthew and I disagree, he will say, 'God, you always have to be right!' I found this really hurtful and worried about how bad it was of me to always want to be right. Then I really thought about it and realised that the entire point of an argument is that we *both* think we are right and we are trying to change the other's mind. If I'm going to put forward an opinion, of course I think I'm right! I wouldn't be putting it forward if I thought I was wrong. If you think I'm wrong, change my mind! To me, that's a really good discussion. When I go out to a dinner party and I'm sat next to another mental fencer, I really enjoy it. At times it's made Matthew cross his legs.

'Tell me why? This is great! Disagree with me! Amazing!' I say.

Above: Gaby, me, my mum and Caroline. Building bridges. I
was so excited at the time to have my two mummies together
on my wedding day and was looking forward to the future.
I would never have guessed that six months later
I would never see my mum again.

Left: 29 June 2000. My bridesmaids and my sisters (*from left to right*: Clare, Caroline, Milly and Jane). (*Johnny Boylan*)

Below: The kiss. (*Johnny Boylan*)

Left: Me and Soz in St. Tropez. She's *my* person.

Above: What would Olive do?! *(Sarah Clark Photography)*

Below: Finding true peace at Disney. Me and Georgie.

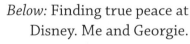

Above: My Milly.

Above: Me at eight and a half months pregnant with Chester. He was 10lbs 2oz. *(gettyimages)*

Below: The night I didn' present the Radio 2 award Hilarious. *(gettyimages*

Left: My last night presenting *Big Brother* after eleven years. *(gettyimages)*

Right: Me and cheetahs.
Life at the Extreme, 2016.
(© January 2016 Plimsoll
Productions Limited)

Above: Is anyone bored of
pictures of my stomach yet?!
LOLS!

Right: I love presenting
Long Lost Family with this
guy. My TV husband,
Nicky Campbell.

Right: Pippy welcoming me over the finish line of my 100k race for Action Medical Research, my annual bike ride.

Left: Me and Greg Whyte after Lake Windermere. I would literally walk over hot coals for this man.

Above: At the finish line of my epic Sport Relief challenge. *(gettyimages)*

My dad, my hero

Left: Mother and son. The look of love.

Below: Daddy and daughter. I'll always be a daddy's girl.

Above: Me and Matthew. My rock.

For me, one of the worst things in the world is apathy. Inaction and apathy are crippling to human life. You don't need to go out and become a Greenham Common activist or a militant anything, but please have an opinion. If you don't have an opinion, think really hard and form an opinion. Get involved. Start something. Join something. Go somewhere. Choose something. If you disagree with somebody, even if everybody else seems to be agreeing with them, say it.

'Sorry'

I think 'sorry' is a really powerful word. When it is said with true meaning, anything can be forgiven.

Firstly, when I want to say sorry to somebody, I make sure it's really from the heart and that I mean it. Any hint of untruth or sarcasm or 'Sorreee!' just has the opposite effect. If the kids do that to each other, I say, 'That's not acceptable because it doesn't feel like a real sorry.'

Secondly, I try never to say 'but' after a sorry (or after 'I love you' either, but that's another story). The minute you say the word 'but' after anything, you've just taken away what you said before.

Thirdly, I try to make eye contact and just say it.

Fourthly, I try not to expect immediate forgiveness. It's got to be an unconditional sorry. It can't be 'Well, I'm taking it back if you're not gonna forgive me.' Sometimes if you've done something really awful, it's not going to be something that can be forgiven immediately, but sorry is a start. A really good start. Sometimes you have to say it a few times before you're forgiven.

Fifthly, actions speak louder than words. Saying 'I'm sorry' is great, and so is behaving like you're sorry. What I mean by that is that I try to show in my behaviour that I'm contrite.

I say sorry all the time. 'That play was really important to you. It was in my diary but I completely forgot, I am so sorry!' 'Matthew, I was upset about something to do with work and took it out on you when I shouted. I'm sorry.' I say it all the time because I don't have a problem saying sorry. It doesn't make me a lesser person.

'Sorry' is one of the most important words in a relationship. Some guys have a real issue with saying it, and I think it's to do with being an alpha male. They think that saying sorry will demean them in some way or mean that they have lost an argument. That could not be further from the truth. I think that owning a mistake and apologising for it makes someone a much stronger person, and I think it's a brilliant and sometimes a brave thing to do.

I don't recall anyone ever apologising to me as a kid, but I say sorry all the time with mine. There was one time, with my youngest, Chester, that I had to really think to find the right words for a sorry.

Chester didn't have a dummy, he didn't suck his thumb, he had a 'nu-nu'. This nu-nu was his everything. It was a weird, really soft cat thing with fleecy tentacles that he could suck. We had fifteen of them, on rotation, so that we could wash them, but I'd have to rub the stinky nu-nu onto the newly washed nu-nu so there'd be a tiny bit of stink on it, otherwise he didn't like them. I'm telling you, these things were rancid.

Anyway, he got to about six and we went on holiday and forgot the nu-nu! He didn't sleep the first night but the rest of the holiday was fine and after that we decided to get rid of the nu-nu because the dentist had warned us that sucking on the tentacle was making his front teeth come forward and that it would be much better if the nu-nu went. So I took the two nu-nus that were the least chewed, washed them, and hid them in his keepsake box (we call them 'ooh-aah boxes') on the top shelf of his cupboard.

'We've lost the nu-nus, I can't find them,' I said, and he cried and cried. But one sleepless night later he got over it and we never had a nu-nu again.

About a year ago, when he was eight, we were going through everybody's ooh-aah boxes, to make sure it was all stuff we really wanted, and Chester spotted his nu-nus! He just looked at me.

'These are my nu-nus,' he said, picking them up.

I was speechless, cursing myself for not moving them. If he'd found them a couple of years later, he wouldn't have cared.

'I loved these. What are they doing here? You told me that they'd gone. You told me that they were lost,' he said, looking at me with eyes that said 'You told me a lie.'

It wasn't one of those situations where I could just say, 'I did it for your own good, Chester. Forget about it.' I could see that he was thinking, 'She told me a lie.' It made me think about my own mum. She told me she was coming back and she never came back again. It made it hard to ever trust her. I needed to explain properly to Chester why this lie was important. So we sat down and I thought really carefully.

'Chester, the dentist had said that we needed to get rid of the nu-nu because it was affecting your teeth. Because you'd forgotten it on holiday, we knew that you could manage without it, but if it was still in the house, you would never have been able to get to sleep without it. If we'd thrown it away, you would have been so angry with us. So this way we did tell a little white lie, and white lies are lies that aren't meant to hurt you, but we felt it was for your own good. This way, you get to keep your nu-nu for ever but you don't need it any more.'

He sat there and really thought about it.

'I'm really sorry I lied to you,' I said. 'I did it because I thought it was in your best interests. I hope you understand.'

He thought about it for a bit. He looked at the nu-nus and then he sucked on one defiantly.

'That's okay,' he finally said. 'Actually, it tastes disgusting.'

A heartfelt sorry goes a very, very long way.

Do things together

Matthew's a really keen mountain-biker and when he said he'd take me biking I thought it would be something great we could do together, even though I hadn't ridden a bike since I was twelve. So he took me out and I was crying within five minutes. We were at the top of this sort of bomb crater in Surrey and he disappeared down into it, over logs and branches, and I just froze. This is a very boy thing; sometimes they do just love throwing you in the deep end.

A few minutes into the bike ride I was absolutely flipping furious. I was cycling along this track and I couldn't see him in front of me. 'Where's he gone? Bastard! He's hiding some-where, or he's just gone off without me. He's just left me alone.' Then I heard, 'Help! Help!' and I thought he was mucking me about. 'Help!' I looked over the edge and he'd fallen off the track and was on his back with his bicycle on top of him. He'd slipped down a steep slope and been stopped by a tree. If I'm really honest, I had a quick, internal giggle . . . but then I sprang into action and helped get him out.

So I never really took to mountain biking, and for the first few years of our relationship his biking was a very testoster-one-fuelled thing. He road-biked too. I just didn't get it. I'd sort of titter behind my hand when I saw him go off wearing all that tight Lycra, I thought it was hysterical. But I also saw how much it meant to him and a part of me wanted to share that with him.

Then about six years ago I was asked to do a challenge for Sport Relief – to cycle from John O'Groats to Land's End. Me and five other people were going to cycle from the top of Scot-land to the tip of Cornwall, over four days, twenty-four hours a day, each of us cycling in two-hour shifts but really pelting it, otherwise we wouldn't make it in time. The weather was likely to be brutal (it was the beginning of March), and I knew I would need to get fit. So I started training and, finally, there I was wearing all the tight Lycra that I'd always teased Matthew about.

For the four days of the challenge we all travelled on a bus, cycling in turn – it was such good fun. We would be woken in the middle of the night and have to get into our kit really quietly so as not to wake anyone up. I was in Glencoe in the Scottish Highlands for one of my stretches, I remember. It was two o'clock in the morning, the ice had melted off the road but the Highlands were covered in snow. In the light of a full moon, the snow looked blue as far as I could see. It was minus fifteen degrees, and my co-rider (we had professional cyclists with us the whole journey, they were doing six hours at a time, and were crazy amazing) got hypothermia and had to get back on the bus, so I said, 'I'll just carry on.' That was probably one of the most magical hour and a halves I've ever had. I was on my own, cycling in the Highlands with all this blue snow every- where, and I thought, 'I would never choose to go out on a bike ride at two o'clock in the morning in the Highlands, but it's so desolate and so eerie and all the snow is shining like crystals. This is magical.' The night-time rides were my favourites. They were the time when I'd look at the countryside and I'd think, 'No one ever cycles through the countryside at this time of night ... magic'

By the end of those four days that was it, I was an absolute road bike obsessive. It's been so bonding for me and Matthew to sit in the front of the car together and say, 'Ooh, look at that hill. That would be a really nice one to ride up,' and the kids will be in the back groaning, 'Oh no, not you as well, Mum!'

I became a total bike bore and now it's something that

Matthew and I can really enjoy doing together. It's important to have things like that. When we've been in marriage guidance counselling, that's something that comes up: you need to find things that you can share. Matthew and I love going to the cinema but I remember our therapist slightly laughed at that: 'It's not ideal as you don't actually speak to each other!'

Don't let your relationship get to the point where you don't want to spend time together. That is the kiss of death. I've learned over the years of our marriage that you have to spend time alone together to stop you ever not wanting to be alone together. If you're not alone together (no kids, no friends, no TV) you can't be alone together when the kids have left home, that's it. Matthew and I always try to make time to be together away from the kids, especially if either of us has been away or has been through a particularly frantic work period. When we don't spend time alone, we really notice it because we argue more. So we'll go for a long bike ride, or spend a night away, or even just go to the cinema. It doesn't have to be a candlelit dinner, staring into each other's eyes and discussing the deepest issues in our relationship, it's just having fun together and feeling close.

When you've got kids and life's busy, it is vital to go out with your husband and leave the kids behind sometimes. Matthew and I have started walking the dogs together in the morning. It's just fifteen minutes but it's time on our own ... which means that, one day, we will have a ... smokin'-hot empty nest! (See below.)

*

Smokin'-hot empty nest

The way to avoid the empty-nest syndrome is to have such a smoking-hot relationship that when the kids leave home you'll say, 'Whoopee, let's travel! Let's go rambling around Great Britain. Let's sail the world.' It's the time to do the stuff that you've been missing out on all those years you've been dedicating to your kids. Go do that.

Empty-nest syndrome happens when we, as parents, invest so much in our kids that our relationship plays second fiddle. I want my kids to have all the love and the time and the nurture that I can give, but the danger in forgetting about your relationship is that the kids leave home and then you don't know the person that you're living with any more. You've drifted apart.

OMG, Michael Heppell (he of *How to Be Brilliant* fame) has got the best relationship of any couple I have ever known. They took a year off recently and just sort of hung out. They really listen to each other. They're hugely respectful of each other. They work together. They spend a lot of time together. They've raised two really great kids who are a testament to their fantastic relationship. When the kids left home, the parents just got closer. They kept their relationship alive and, very kindly, they wrote their top five tips for a great marriage (and a smokin'-hot empty nest) for me to put in this book.

*

Michael and Christine's marriage tips

Know your roles and take responsibility

Responsibility: the ability to respond. Because we work together *and* live together we established that it was important for each of us to take responsibility and have the final say in specific areas of our lives. In theory this idea was simple but initially making it work required some tongue-biting and counting to ten. Now we're clear on our roles and who makes those final decisions.

Manners maketh the man

We always say 'please' and 'thank you'. It's easy to become complacent, so saying a sincere 'thank you' is great for your relationship. For example, if your partner has cooked for you, say 'thank you' and pay a compliment about the food before you've even tasted it. Remember to say 'thank you' after you've eaten too.

And don't think your partner can receive too many compliments. 'You look great in those jeans' never gets boring.

Aim for a level 3 relationship

A level 1 relationship is 'What can I get out of this?' It's where most relationships start. You find someone attractive, you want them in your life and when you get them life is just peachy.

A level 2 relationship is 'I'll do this for you, but I expect you to do that for me.' This is where most couples progress to and too many stall. There's nothing wrong with 'You went out on Friday with your mates, so I'm going out on Saturday with mine,' but you don't need to make deals at home.

A level 3 relationship is 'Your needs are my needs.' In other words, you put your partner's needs first and you do whatever it takes to help them to fulfil their needs. This selfless approach is challenging but massively rewarding to both parties.

Develop your own relationship language

'It's in the diddly-doddly' means nothing to anyone else, but in our house we'd know exactly where to look. Shops are shibi-dies, spingers are fingers, panta is underwear (male and female) and the buttons can, and often does, mean anything. Developing a language that only you share always makes you smile.

Don't let your kids divide and conquer

Children are a great blessing in a relationship, whether you have your own or you borrow some from your friends/family. But they can be little sods too. It doesn't take them long before their conniving little brains work out that if they can't get their way with one parent, they'll try with the other. Even if one parent thinks a certain behaviour is acceptable and the other doesn't, a united response is vital.

TNTs

Tiny noticeable touches are normally associated with five-star hotels, but we like to do tiny noticeable toothbrushes. Whoever is first in the bathroom, morning or night, puts the toothpaste on both toothbrushes. We've done this for our whole marriage and we never tire of seeing our toothbrush by the sink with a little squeeze of toothpaste lovingly applied.

5

How Not to Mess Up
Your Kids

Be nice to pregnant women

I want to talk about the language that we use about pregnant women. Because when I was pregnant I was super vulnerable, hormonal, sensitive, and so aware of protecting myself and my little bump from everything. Even loud noises would make me hug my bump and give it a little rub and say, 'It's all going to be okay.' You're nurturing and protecting right from the start. From the minute I conceived, I could sense it.

I was in love with my very pregnant body but I did struggle in the first three months. My best feature, my hot bit, is my stomach. As people probably know, I get it out all the time. My thighs and my bum are quite big but because of my good flat stomach I can get away with them. For the first three months, four months, my tummy went a bit jellified. When I was about nine weeks I went to see an acupuncturist and I said, 'Aww, look, I've got a little belly already,' and she said, 'I hate to tell you this but the baby hasn't popped out of your pelvis yet. That is just your belly preparing, but it's not in there. It doesn't pop out until thirteen weeks.' I was like, 'Oh my God, the baby's still in my pelvis? That's not the baby? Oh, this is going to be bad.'

The pregnancy usually starts showing at five or six months, but I was already the size of a small country by then. My little sister's pregnant now and she's so perfect. She's got very skinny legs and looks like somebody's put a football up her T-shirt. I did not look like that. I looked like somebody had put me in a fat suit. It got to the point where the only footwear I could wear was flip-flops and after a while even flip-flops were too tight. I had to wear Crocs.

So, this is what I've learned about talking to pregnant women:

Rule 1: When I started talking about my pregnancy, I noticed how many people said to me, 'Ooh, you're quite big, aren't you?' Argggghhhh! NEVER SAY THAT TO A PREGNANT WOMAN. When you're sensitive and full of hormones and already feeling quite insecure about the way that you look, for somebody to come up to you and your beautiful pregnant belly and say, 'Ooh, you're quite big, aren't you?' *is literally the worst thing*!

Rule 2: I had people saying to me, 'Are you sure you're not having twins? Ha ha ha ha ha.' It's not f***ing funny. I know I'm not having twins. This is just my size.

Rule 3: Sometimes people would say, 'Ooh, you're really bloom-ing, aren't you?' We can see through 'blooming'. It means 'massively fat'. And yes, I am one of those people who balloons and shrinks, balloons and shrinks, but was I thrilled when people consistently told me how big I was? *No.*

The only people who were positive about everything were my beautiful midwives. They always told me that I was the perfect size, that I looked amazing, that I was doing a great job, that I was carrying the baby brilliantly, and I felt so happy and energised ... And then somebody would ask to rub my tummy and say, 'You're quite big, aren't you?' I'd just think, 'Shut up with your "quite big" comments. Piss off, all of you!'

Then, as I was coming nearer to the time of delivery, it started with the 'Oh my God, good luck with that. I had the worst birth ever' comments. *Why do people do that?* Based on how many women shared their horrific birth stories with me, I would guess that everybody had horrific births – but it was only those who'd had a dreadful time and needed to share it. *Just don't do it!* I'm really sorry if you had an awful experience but share it with somebody who's got a four-year-old. Don't share it with a pregnant woman.

If I'm in a supermarket or in the street or on holiday and we see a pregnant woman, my kids say, 'Oh my God, quick, move Mummy away. Pregnant lady coming. MOVE MUMMY AWAY! PREGNANT LADY COMING!'

It doesn't ever work. I walk straight up to the pregnant stranger and say, 'Excuse me? When are you due? You look so beautiful. How gorgeous. I just wanted to let you know that I had a great experience with all of my children and I loved giving birth. I just wanted to let you know that.' Then I walk away. Sometimes the women look at me like I'm really odd, but I don't care because I think they are probably getting all the horror stories and I want to counter that. Every single pregnant woman I've spoken to has said the same thing, so this is a message to women:

Please *don't tell a pregnant woman that you had an awful time giving birth.*

Just suck it up and keep it to yourself because that lady might be enjoying being pregnant ... but she'll sure as hell be absolutely bricking it after you've told her your horror story, and fear is the number-one closer of the cervix and blocker of birth. The minute you're all feared up everything shuts down, your cervix is clamped together like a clam, and you're just not going to be in a good place to give birth. Women perpetuate this level of fear by making you so frightened about it, right up until the minute you give birth, that by the time you give birth you're thinking, 'I don't want to do this! I don't want to do this! Just give me a C-section. I just want an epidural. I just want to lie down and read *OK!* magazine. Tell me when it's come out.' Fear in childbirth is awful, so give a pregnant woman positive vibes and you're giving her the best possible chance of having a good birth.

*

Don't judge anyone for the birth they want (in fact, just don't judge anyone EVER)

Giving birth was the most amazing experience of my entire life. Every time.

When I got pregnant the first time, I was going down the private route, a la-di-dah private hospital where they had a neonatal unit. I was thinking, 'Safety first!' I'd see the obstetrician there and he was always worrying about things because that's what obstetricians do – they're doctors, they are looking for the problems.

When I was about twenty-two weeks I had some friends over called Annabel and Barnabus. Annabel started telling me about her births. She was telling me about how much she'd loved giving birth and what an amazing experience she'd had, at home with two midwives, and as I listened to her I found myself wanting to cry. I'd *never* heard anybody talk about birth like that. The minute people found out I was pregnant they'd say, 'Oh my God, it was horrific! I tore from here to here! I had to have an episiotomy. My waters broke in Sainsbury's! I haemorrhaged! I nearly died! The baby nearly died ...' I was so flipping terrified! So when she told me that she loved giving birth I started grilling her.

'Why did you love giving birth?'

'It's the most empowering thing I've ever done.'

'But I don't understand, doesn't it hurt like hell?'

'Yes, it hurts, but I'm so proud of myself. We got through it together. We laughed.'

'You what?'

'We laughed.'

'You laughed? Are you kidding me?'

'I'm going to give you my midwife's name and number. Call her. Let me know how it goes.'

So I called up this woman, Caroline Flint, who I now know is a legend in the birthing world, and I waddled off to see her.

'You look lovely,' was the first thing she said to me.

'Thank you. I'm quite big,' I said.

'No, you're absolutely the right size,' she replied.

Everything she said made sense and made me feel cherished and amazing. She was an independent midwife, so I was paying for her services, but the NHS also has fantastic midwives who will do home deliveries. She explained that they would do all my check-ups and would only send me to a doctor if they felt there was something to worry about. 'We'll look after you. That's what midwives do,' she said. It was a completely different approach to what I'd signed up for at the hospital.

I went home and talked it through with Matthew who was very resistant to the idea. We went online and armed ourselves with statistics and together we came up with the decision to stay booked into the hospital but to keep the midwives who would stay with me when I was in labour at home and then, if I wanted to go to hospital I could, but if not I could stay at home. He was happy with that.

So that was it. I was off. I never saw another doctor. Every experience I had with the midwives was lovely. I read a book called *Spiritual Midwifery* by Ina May Gaskin (the *most incredible* woman who has pioneered the natural birth movement in the US) that Annabel had given to me and I learned a lot from that. My favourite page is advice for mothers at the time of birth.

> Keep your sense of humor ... If you can't be a hero, you can at least be funny whilst being a chicken.
>
> *Ina May Gaskin*

Here are some other brilliant quotes from this extraordinary woman, who said of the commune she started with her husband in Tennessee, 'We were actually making our own culture of birth in which fear was not going to be a big part.'

> It is important to keep in mind that our bodies must work pretty well, or there wouldn't be so many humans on the planet.

> Be nice to people around you, because they're all concerned about you.

> Many of our problems in ... maternity care stem from the fact that we leave no room for recognizing when nature is smarter than we are.

> Human female bodies have the same potential to give birth well as aardvarks, lions, rhinoceri, elephants, moose, and water buffalo.

Even if it has not been your habit throughout your life so far, I recommend that you learn to think positively about your body.

Birth doesn't happen the same way around surgeons, medically trained doctors, as it does around sympathetic women.

Whenever and however you give birth, your experience will impact your emotions, your mind, your body, and your spirit for the rest of your life.

If a woman doesn't look like a goddess during labor, then someone isn't treating her right.

Good beginnings make a positive difference in the world, so it is worth our while to provide the best possible care for mothers and babies throughout this extraordinarily influential part of life.

When we as a society begin to value mothers as the givers and supporters of life, then we will see social change in ways that matter.

Another bit of advice, which a friend of mine called Jamie Cato gave me, was to keep repeating the mantra 'It's safe to open even more.' Sometimes the pain gets super intense (or the 'interesting feelings' get intense, as Ina May puts it) and I had to keep thinking, 'It's safe pain, it's safe pain, it's safe to open even more' and it really helped me relax.

I had a really, really long labour with Holly – thirty-six

hours – and I wanted to give up so many times, but the midwives kept me going, kept me positive. We laughed a lot. I got into some really undignified positions and wafted around the house with no clothes on, but it was definitely one of the most fantastic experiences of my whole life. Tilly was super short and mega-intense, ending up in a beautiful water birth, and Chester was just about perfect, also a lovely water birth. It was like 'Goldilocks and the Three Bears' but all of them were midwife-led and all of them were beautiful experiences. That feeling of pride, of wanting to take your baby and stand in the middle of your lawn holding them up like Simba in *The Lion King*, that will never leave me (my village would have been a bit worried seeing me naked on the lawn holding up a baby . . . but you know what I mean). I wanted to run fifteen marathons after I'd given birth. I felt fantastic.

People got quite annoyed with me for wanting natural births because they thought I was putting my babies in danger. We did our own research and decided that it was just as safe, if not a tiny bit safer, having a baby at home if you're low risk and you've got an experienced midwife with you. People have to do their own research and make their own decisions, but they should be allowed to decide what feels right for them. My lesson is not to judge anybody by the birth that they want. If you're having a baby, go for the birth you want. Don't let anybody tell you that you *should* be doing this or *shouldn't* be doing that. I've got a friend who read *Hello!* magazine throughout her entire birth, and when they said push she pushed, and then she had a baby and she loved it. She can't recommend that approach highly enough. I have another friend who was absolutely terrified of giving birth and she had an elective caesarean. Just have the birth you want and stuff the judgers!

Rushing and expelling

The wording around birth is all wrong.

Most people say that women have 'contractions' and then 'push' the baby out. I don't, and nor would you if you'd read birth guru Ina May Gaskin's book *Spiritual Midwifery*.

The word 'contraction' gives the wrong idea. It makes you think of things coming together, shrinking, closing, clinging on, whereas Ina May Gaskin calls it a 'rush'. I love that! It's a rush of energy, a rush that opens and surges forward, which is a much better picture to have in your head while giving birth than 'contracting'.

Then there's 'pushing', the bit you always see in TV dramas and hospital soaps, with sweaty women being told to push as they make noises like a weightlifter heaving a ten-ton bar over his head. 'How will I know when to push?' was my biggest question when I was first pregnant. I was thinking, 'If it's something I need to do, then I need to know when to start.'

In fact, you don't push the baby out at all. The rushes in your body are getting the baby out for you. They are ... what's the best word? *Ejecting* the baby? No: *expelling*. Unless you have an epidural, your body does it by itself. That's why actresses who have never had babies often get it slightly wrong and do a lot of straining.

So, instead of contractions and pushing, I say that a rush expels the baby. Thanks Ina May. (I came up with 'expelling', but I'll give Ina May 'the rush'). It's like something from Harry Potter, isn't it? 'Expelliarmus! Get the baby out!'

When you have a baby, everything changes

I was very much into planning, planning, planning ... Planning getting pregnant, which month I was going to get pregnant, because I had to plan my pregnancies around *Big Brother* (all my babies are born in September – hilarious. In December I'd say, 'We can start trying,' and bish, bash, bosh ... preggers); planning my entire life, visualising and planning every step of the way. What I hadn't planned was that having a baby changes everything. Having Holly changed me as a human being.

When I got pregnant I was sure I'd go back to work three months after the birth. I told my agent to book me stuff for then; but when Holly was born, it was like a love bomb went off in my life and I just wanted to stay at home for ever. I never wanted to work again. I was lucky because I could work just two or three days a week, but it was still really, *really* hard. With each subsequent child I took more time off but it's a TOTAL life-changer. It robbed me of all my ambition.

Every mother is different and my experience is not going to be somebody else's, but I do remember when Matthew went to the pub for the first time after Holly was born. I said, 'I'll come with . . . Oh . . . I can't, we've got a baby. I've got to stay at home. Hang on a minute, what happens when I want to go out? Well, actually, I don't want to go out.' Everything was so different!

It changed our relationship too, and I think it's good to brace yourself for that. Men . . . listen up! You need to understand that you haven't lost your wife, you have gained a family. I think some men mourn not being the centre of their wife's world any more. Having said that, the first six months for any man is tough, because they're not getting much out of the baby unless they're a real baby person, which is quite rare, so it's difficult. For me, I was put on this earth to make babies. I just was a bit obsessed with my babies. It was quite tough on Matthew. Thank you, Matthew.

I think when I had my first child, perhaps because of what my own mother was like, I put this pressure on myself to be perfect. I was quite rigid with myself, because of this need I had to get everything right. Matthew must have thought, 'I married this really fun, nightclubbing loon and she's turned into a rather uptight, extremely exhausted mum.' I was terrified, I think.

All I can say to new parents is, 'It's all gonna be fine!'

Having looked after my first child, slightly on edge, the second didn't get as much attention as the first and had to just muck in, and she was absolutely fine as well. It made no difference. As long as you love your baby, take care of it, feed it, it'll be absolutely fine.

*

Love and boundaries

Katie Ross-Russell, my friend from school, has four girls who are all gorgeous. She was about six years ahead of me in having her babies, so when I had my first I called her and said, 'Oh my God, I've got a baby. Yours are amazing. I have a girl. Please give me advice.' She was a social worker at the time and worked with so many different families, she'd had the best parents ever, and was, in my eyes, the most incredible parent to her children.

'Please, just tell me how to do this!' I said.

'That's really easy, Davina. Love and boundaries.'

'That's it?!' I was expecting some epic list of rules: this is the time they've got to go to bed, this is what they've got to eat, this is how many videos in foreign languages you need to show them to help them be multi-lingual, etc.

'No, none of that. All that matters is that your child knows you love them by you telling them, hugging and touching them.'

'Okay, I get the love bit,' I said. I think most people do that naturally anyway. I loved cuddling my babies. 'But talk me through boundaries.'

'Never lay down a boundary that you can't absolutely adhere to,' said Katie.

I've stuck to that advice, although I've put some boundaries in place that I've massively regretted afterwards! I remember when one of my kids was being particularly out of order. She was four and we were in Australia and had been invited to a party with loads of friends. This was going to be our only opportunity to see them.

'If you do that again, you're not going to this party', I said. ... And she did it again.

'Why did I say that?!' I thought. 'I really want to go to the party and now I can't!'

It was painful but we didn't go, and she understood pretty quickly that I always stand by my boundaries. That way, a child will learn that when Mummy says, 'If you do this there will be consequences,' she means it. If I don't follow through, I'm basically saying, 'My word means nothing and you can walk all over me'. So that was the first and most valuable child-rearing lesson anybody's ever taught me.

Routines?

I hated Gina Ford. Sorry. Her books made me feel really frightened about parenting. All her rigid routines, timed to the minute, one-size-fits-all ... I think parenting's got to be quite organic. With the best intentions, sometimes too much advice from other people can make mothers feel a bit helpless. I'm all about empowering mums to listen to themselves and their children.

Other than 'love and boundaries' and making sure they had a good nap every day, I didn't follow any routines except for having lengthy bathtimes and bedtimes. As a working mum, that was the bit I missed most, so after supper we would have lovely long baths and then we'd all play or read together. After that, each child would get an individual bedtime with a story, a prayer and a cuddle. Their own quiet time with Mummy. It was precious.

I think because my childhood was quite chaotic, it made me bring a lot of tradition into my house. 'This is what we do at bedtime.' It was very calming and was always really important to me and for the kids when they were toddlers.

Fairy dust

When the kids were younger, all of them at some point during their life had nasty nightmares, sometimes so bad that they'd really cry out, so I made up this thing called fairy dust. I hope they don't read this book because when they find out it's made up they'll be devastated. Anyway, fairy dust is something that the fairies deposit in my pockets. It's a limitless amount. I've always got it if I need it. It's just there by magic. I don't know how it gets there but it is there.

At night, when I was putting them to bed, I'd pull a little handful of fairy dust out of my pocket. Sometimes I asked if they could feel it as I sprinkled, and they said that they could. I'd sprinkle it over their heads and say:

> *'Fairies, fairies, warm and bright,*
> *Keep my Holly safe tonight.*

Take away her bad dreams [and I'd make a big
sweeping-away hand gesture] *and bring her good,
And help her feel as good as she should.'*

Now, I know that it's appallingly jerky, but it rhymes. Then I'd repeat that last bit: 'Take away her bad dreams and bring her good, and help her feel as good as she should.' I've done that with all of my children, and it's worked. They go to bed thinking that the fairies have taken away the bad dreams and brought good ones. Sometimes Holly and Tilly still ask for it and get all soppy. CUTE!

I think rituals for children are really important. They make them feel safe. Something that you do every night, your thing, it's grounding and heart-warming. I cherished having that when I lived with my granny. Every night, either my granny would come up and tell me a night-night story or my Auntie Sheena would do this thing called 'Snow on the Mountains'. Oh my God, I loved it. I'd lie in bed and she'd pull back the sheet, the eiderdown and the blanket (these were the days before duvets) and I'd be in my nightie and she'd go, 'They were up in the mountains and they were walking around and then suddenly it started snowing and this big veil of snow came down.' She'd pull the sheet over me and it would float down over my face, and then the eiderdown would come down, much heavier: 'snow on the mountains And then the last blanket would come down and she'd go, 'Then springtime came,' and she'd peel back the blankets and tickle me. It was amazing. Some nights my grandpa Mickey put me to bed, and he would always give me sums to do. He absolutely loved maths and he made me love maths too.

Holly always really struggled to get to sleep because she'd be thinking at ninety miles an hour, so we used to do a count-down. I'd start at ten and say something like 'Picture yourself on a beach. You can hear the water swishing. Nine. The sand is very warm. Eight. There are dolphins in the sea,' and so on until we got to one and I'd go 'Night-night' and walk out. To Tilly I say the Serenity Prayer, which is:

> **'God grant me the serenity to accept the things I cannot change, courage to change the things I can, and wisdom to know the difference.'**

To Chester I read the prayer that had been in a frame above my Great-Auntie Patty's bed (Pippy's sister). When Great-Auntie Patty died she left it to me and I put it next to Chester's bed. It's a lovely prayer. It begins 'Each daisy on its little sod' (the word sod always made me giggle).

> *Each daisy on its little sod*
> *Is made and known and loved by God,*
> *So I may rest and fold my hands,*
> *For all my thoughts God understands,*
> *And I may be in perfect peace,*
> *For sleep shall be my soul's release.*
> *And like the sun my heart will shine*
> *For all the love of God is mine.*

Don't expect perfection

People I love have made mistakes or hurt or upset me, but I have had to remember that no one's perfect. The only unforgiveable thing would be if somebody shtupped my husband. That would be a hard one. But people make mistakes and they cock up (I am the queen of cock-ups).

> *To have extraordinarily high expectations of people, to seek perfection in friends and family and partners, is to invite misery, because no one's perfect and people will always disappoint you.*

I'm very forgiving with my kids. If they make a mistake, do something wrong, forget something, I'll always tell them not to worry, I know they didn't mean it. When I make a mistake, like missing a match because I completely forgot, they say the same to me.

Children become what you tell them they are

Another incredibly important lesson I've learned is that my children will become what I call them. So if I say to my kids, 'You're so bad, you're so naughty,' they will rise to that label and be even naughtier. I've worked really, really hard not to label my children because, like me, they are fluid beings, always changing and developing.

I think the main labels that we give our kids are the place-in-the-family labels. 'Oh, you're the baby.' 'You're the eldest.' 'You're the middle.' I don't buy into that. If you say to a child, 'Well, of course, you're the middle child,' they'll just go, 'Oh, amazing, I've got an excuse for any kind of errant behaviour because I'm the middle child.' We've all got crosses to bear for where we came in our family.

Something my kids have taught me is that they cherish my approval above everything else. So if I say to them, 'I'm really proud of you,' it makes their heart sing – you can see it. If they've been quite difficult or a bit out of sorts, I'll find something they've done well, even if it's absolutely tiny, and praise that. So I won't say, 'It wasn't very nice when you did this,' or 'That was a bit mean . . .' I'll ignore all that and say, 'Tonight I asked you to come upstairs for your bath and you came straight away. I really appreciate that. Thank you.' That might be the *only* thing that day that I could thank them for, but they'll go to bed thinking, 'Mummy was proud of me for doing that. I'll deliver more of that in the future.'

Often I will praise the nice things they've done for each other. That enforces sibling harmony – a very precious thing.

Noticing the little things they do well builds confidence and self-esteem.

One of mine got 7 per cent in an exam once, they were horrified.

'That's not bad. Do you think you can do better?' I said.

'Yeah, I do.'

'Me too. Let's do it! Let's aim for a little bit higher. Do you want some support?' I said. Not, 'Are you disappointed? We're disappointed.' The next exam they got 17 per cent and I said, 'YAAAY let's just aim for a little bit more next time.' The next exam they got 56 per cent and we were literally flick-flacking across the lawn.

That's not to say I was *never* Shouty Mum. I was Shouty Mum when I was pre-menstrual and in the mornings. Oh my God, I was so shouty!

'Come on, everybody! Come downstairs! We've got to get in the car!' Sometimes, when they were in primary school, I would drop them off at school and start crying. Then one day, another mum said, 'Have you tried setting your alarm clock twenty minutes earlier?'

'Do you think that would make a difference?' I said, incredulous.

'A massive difference.'

So I did as she advised, and no more shouting. I haven't shouted since. I was up, dressed, we had plenty of time for breakfast . . . Calm. Now I always aim to leave the house five minutes before I need to, so when I get the 'I don't know where my shoes are' or 'I'm supposed to take in food today for Harvest Festival', I have five minutes to sort it out. That was a fantastic piece of advice.

*

Most children rise to responsibility

The more responsibility you give children, the more they rise to the occasion.

I've given Holly and Tilly a debit card (debit *not* credit!) for the pocket money they earn doing chores.

I originally thought I shouldn't give my kids money because they wouldn't know what to do with it. They'd go completely mad, like I did at seventeen, and that it would be an absolute disaster. The opposite was true. I would give my kids appropriate amounts of pocket money to see how responsible they are with it. And they have been. Far from being frivolous or buying stupid stuff, Holly and Tilly have been super sensible with their money and they save up for things. I'm about to give Holly her entire clothing budget for the year. It will mean that she will be making decisions about her clothing, like 'Do I save up for UGG boots or do I get the *fake* UGG boots that are half the price and look very similar?' It means that if we buy her a pair of real UGG boots for Christmas she's mega-mega-mega grateful because she knows how much they cost. So I'm giving her massive financial responsibility. If she blows it on something frivolous, she'll run out of money and she won't be able to buy a winter coat, and I'll say 'Well, you spent your money, you'll have to wait till your birthday,' and I'll stick to it. That's how you learn. I know I sound brutal, but even though I have money my kids still need to appreciate the value of money. When they have to save up to pay for things or they can't get something straight away, they appreciate what we give them even more.

Of course, some kids find it much harder to respond to this sort of parenting. Lots of kids have behavioural issues, like ADHD, or they're on the autistic spectrum; then obviously it's about seeking out the right kind of help for you and your child. I don't want to make parenting sound all peaches-and-cream and easy as anything. It hasn't been. Every child is different, and these are just some tips or hints I've picked up along the way, but they are in no way meant to make anybody feel inadequate if their child doesn't respond to them. Parenting can be a really tough job and we all just have to get through it the best way that we can.

What would Olive do?

None of us want to look silly in front of other people, we can all be a bit self-conscious, teenagers in particular, and whenever any of my children are worried about something, or have to perform, we ask: 'What would Olive do?' It's an actual thing in our family, named after one of my daughter's friends, Olive, who is like a glorious character from an Enid Blyton *Malory Towers* book. She's hysterically funny and *so* gutsy. Her whole family are really lovely and confident and totes could not care less about what people think of them. If there's something they want to try, they'll just give it a go.

It all started when my daughter had to do cartwheels and

handstands in her gymnastics class. I've never been able to do them, I'm just genetically not predisposed to cartwheels and handstands, and although being able to do them might bring me joy, it's okay for me not to be able to do them; but for my daughter it's not. Other people can do them. She wants to be able to do them. So she'd been practising, but she was having a tough time, the lesson was looming, and she was really frightened of looking silly.

Then I began wondering what her friend Olive would do. We sat down and talked it through. Olive would walk in, so confident, and she'd have a go. If it went wrong, she'd jump up and say, 'I'm really good at these!' She'd make a joke and everybody would laugh with her and think, 'Oh, Olive's hilarious.'

My daughter went to the class and thought, 'What would Olive do?' She styled it out and now it's a thing in our house. Even I ask myself, 'What would Olive do?' ... She gets *me* through things too.

Do not over-reassure your kids

Most kids between ten and thirteen get embarrassed. It might be about performing something at school or doing something sporty that they felt they couldn't do; mine were sometimes embarrassed about me being famous, and especially by my singing and dancing! Double embarrassed if I did it at school!!

But one of my children had a worry that grew. It turned into a bit of anxiety and I didn't know what to do. It started with my sister's death. I think it was a time when my children suddenly realised that people you really, really love are mortal and can disappear. Around the same time we'd seen a robber running down the street with a policewoman chasing him. Now, I'm the sort of person who would step in and *take him down* but I couldn't because I had the three kids with me. I got quite agitated and screamed '*Stop!*' (it was all very dramatic), and me doing that totally freaked out one of my kids. From then on things started getting very tidy in her room. Not OCD, but when she went round to her mates she would tidy and hoover their room before she could sleep in it.

I've got a friend called Dr Tanya Byron, who is literally the cleverest woman I know. She is the Don Corleone of child behaviour and of generally everything. You can ask her a question about anything and she'll give you the best answer ever. I called her and told her that I was worried and she totally understood. Tanya's figured out that I'm a bit of an anxious parent (always too busy trying to be perfect), so she knew exactly what to say. She gave me four key bits of advice.

1. **Don't over-reassure an anxious child** – which was weird. I mean, what a strange thing to not do. Our instinct as parents is to say, 'It's all going to be all right. Nothing bad is ever going to happen to you. I'm going to protect you from

everything and it's all going to be okay.' And quite rightly, Tanya pointed out that you can't guarantee these things and life isn't like that.

2. **Say something closer to the truth**, such as 'Look, sometimes things do happen but we'll cross that bridge when we come to it. We can all get through this together.' That really helps. She suggested we read *What to Do When You Worry too Much*, which is a lovely book by Dawn Huebner for kids around the ages of ten to fourteen. It was really helpful.

3. **Challenge**. Tanya told me to talk about the tidying, not to make it the big elephant in the room that everybody avoids mentioning, and she encouraged me to challenge it. Again, it felt really mean and counter-intuitive, because if cleaning and tidying made my daughter feel better then shouldn't I let her do it as much as she liked? What Tanya explained is that if I let it get too ingrained, the tidying itself could become a bit of an issue. So I'd move things before she went to bed and say, 'Right, you've got to leave that until the morning,' then at breakfast I'd ask if she'd tidied her room and she'd say no. And I'd say, 'Well done!'

4. **Laugh!** Make a joke about it. 'Oh look, your room's very tidy again. Hang on, I'm gonna move this blanket and I'm gonna mess it up!' And we'd all laugh about it. And she'd be like, 'Mummy!' Making a joke stopped it from becoming a big, looming horror.

It took about a year and a half, but then she just started relaxing and I look at her bedroom now and she's definitely grown out of the tidying!

Keep your kid's secrets

As an adult, I understand that secrets are almost impossible to keep. If a girlfriend wants to tell me a secret I always ask if I can tell Matthew, because I find it very hard to keep secrets from him. God, he's like a heat-seeking missile with secrets. If they say no, then I think long and hard whether I want them to tell me. To children, secrets are really, really, REALLY important. If they want to tell me about somebody who's upset them but they don't want me to talk to their mother, and I promise I won't, then I can't, because if my child finds out they'll never tell me anything again. I overheard Tilly saying to a friend of hers, 'My mummy's really good at keeping secrets,' and it was the nicest thing she could have ever said about me.

Tell your kids they can ask you anything (I know, scary!)

OK, PEOPLE – THIS IS ABOUT INTERNET SAFETY.

I told my kids *before* they got to seven or eight that if they ever heard a word that they don't understand and they don't want to look silly at school, just to ask me and I'd tell them what it meant.

'I won't be embarrassed and I won't make you embarrassed and I definitely won't laugh at you or be angry. I will just explain what it is. And I won't be shocked either, because I've heard just about every single word there is. If I don't know what it means, I look it up and tell you,' is what I say to them.

It takes concentration sometimes, but if I ever show them that I am laughing, shocked or angry they will NEVER come to me again.

I learned this from a friend whose son had searched the word 'rape'. She had found him, aged nine, in his room on a laptop, horrified. He'd heard the word on the radio that morning going into school and he'd wanted to understand what it meant. So when we listen to the radio I always ask the kids if they want me to explain something. The other day they were talking about giving out free condoms. I had to explain what condoms were, which was a useful chat to have. It was a really short chat. I explained in age-appropriate language and that was that. Knowledge is power, especially when you're a child. (Also, I learned from this friend not to allow laptops or computers in my kids' bedrooms until they are at least fourteen.)

I remember when one of my kids was in Year 2 there was this funny word 'sexing'. They were talking about people 'sexing' and then they'd giggle. I told them that 'sexing' isn't a word (but I guessed they thought it had something to do with making love or having sex with someone). They'd heard a word a bit wrong and turned it into 'sexing', but they didn't really know what it meant. So I cracked out the book *Mummy Laid an Egg* by Babette Cole – IT'S AWESOME – and we talked about mummies and daddies fitting together. If you leave it as 'sexing' at seven and they're really excited about it and nobody talks about it, then it becomes this fascinating secret thing that is, ooh, so exciting.

Passing on a positive self-image

In my day, when I got my period, it was called 'the curse' and I was made to feel it was an awful cross to bear. Actually, it's a celebration of becoming a woman, a different phase in your life, and I've been able to pass on a much more positive experience to my kids than I had. Obviously I'm not going to share my kids' experience, but the language I use about all things feminine is always positive.

Talk to your kids about sex

I think the best protection I can give my children is knowledge. Knowledge is power. I say this a lot.

I used to worry that talking to my kids about sex would encourage them to go off and do things they shouldn't or weren't ready for. Then I made this fab series for Channel 4 called *Let's Talk Sex*, about whether or not kids should have sex education, and I walked away from that experience absolutely convinced that they should. I learned that education, far from making children sexualised or promiscuous, does quite the opposite. In Holland, where sex education is widely taught in schools from a young age and is directed at both girls and boys, to empower them to make the right choices for their health and happiness, they have one of the lowest teenage pregnancy rates in the world. The highest teenage birth rates are found in Bulgaria, Romania and the United Kingdom.

I got amazing advice doing that documentary. I learned that you only tell kids what is suitable for their ages, in language that's appropriate, but which answers their questions and makes the whole subject normal. When they're young, you don't want to overload them with too much information. Getting age-appropriate books is brilliant, such as *Mummy Laid an Egg*, or *Where Willy Went* and *More and More Rabbits* by Nicholas Allan.

Kids do start figuring it out for themselves. I'm quite lucky because my son has learned so much from his two older sisters. I'm determined that he understands women's issues and that the girls are understanding to men's.

The other day, Chester said, 'Are the girls crying for no reason?' He knows that sometimes girls will have a huge surge of hormones and feel massively emotional but that it won't be about anything in particular. I thought that was the cutest thing, that he understands there are times when girls don't need to have a reason to cry, we just do. Equally, the girls know that if Chester's hurt himself and is about to cry, they don't necessarily have to rush over to give him sympathy because he won't want to make a big deal out of it. He'll try to process it in his own way and is embarrassed by mollycoddling.

As they've got older, I've given the kids more information and armed them with tools such as saying no with grace (see below).

I also go on and on and on and on about the internet, sexting, texting, and how it can all go horribly wrong. Sometimes I send my eldest daughter articles about girls who have been the victims of revenge porn.

'Look,' I say, 'this guy was going out with this girl and he put that on the internet. He loved her once . . . and he still did this. So even when you are REALLY in love, NO pics that you don't want the world to see.'

Me going on about it drives them mad, but hopefully it'll protect them to know about it. Sometimes it's a bit depressing, it feels like robbing them of their innocence, but I'd rather do that than for them to get in a pickle where they feel compromised.

Kids *never* take responsibility for their animals

My kids were *so* excited about getting guinea pigs. If there are any parents reading this book: don't ever believe your kids when they say they will definitely, *definitely* feed and clean out any kind of pet that you have. They're lying. I lied. My kids have lied. They don't do it. If you're happy to clean out that animal cage for the rest of your life then get the guinea pig. Despite all the best intentions in the world, the kids don't do it.

Conflict Resolution

When my kids row, it's sooooo tempting to wade in and fix it, but actually, if I leave them to resolve it, they find a way. They used to fight over who was going to sit in the front seat of the car, and I'd wade in, thinking I was helping, and it would end up being a big battle every morning. Then my friend suggested I let them sort it out themselves. I was a bit cynical. I was sure it would escalate into World War III. Still, I suggested they find a system so we didn't have a fight every single morning. And they did!! Can you believe it?! I was so proud. I told them too!

Conflict resolution is learned by resolving conflict. You can't sort things out if you've never learned how.

Teach your kids everything before they go into 'the tunnel'

My Uncle Simon told me that kids go into 'the tunnel' at around twelve, by which point I need to have taught them everything they need to know to be a good person, because once they're in the tunnel, you can't teach them anything (ain't that the truth). You need to show them how to navigate moral and ethical dilemmas and how to form and voice their opinions before then. Once in the tunnel, they learn through making mistakes. I can gently guide them through these mistakes but I can't stop them making them. I have to be there to pick up the pieces, provide an ear to listen to them, and teach them how to help themselves.

In this phase, it's tempting to say things like 'You're not going out in that,' but our appearance is the one way that we can shock our parents and be independent, so if you don't let your kids express themselves in that way then they'll express themselves in ways we wouldn't want them to do. I used to go clubbing in a skating outfit so short you could see my bum hanging out. I went to a nightclub called Shoom wearing a neoprene body-glove swimming costume, and a pair of Timberlands. Nothing else! I'd go out in thermals or cycling shorts and crop tops all the time (thank God there was no Snapchat then). In fact, I wore next to nothing and I took the train everywhere.

I know the world is a dangerous place and we have to be careful, but rather than telling your kids they can't go out dressed like that, make sure they travel in packs. A pack of girls is pretty intimidating. I always go for 'Let's get everybody round here and you can all go together.'

People say to me, 'Oh my God, how are you going to stop your kids doing drugs?' The answer to that? I don't know. I don't have a magic ex-addict crystal ball. I'm hoping that when they face those problems, they'll make strong and good decisions. They might not. None of us know. I can't be with them all the time (God knows, I wish I could sometimes), but I've got to think, 'I've trusted you enough. I've given you everything you need. You've got the tools. You go out there and you live.' The best thing I can do is, no matter what they come and tell me, never, ever, ever, ever, ever shame them, or they will never come back again. I will never laugh at them. I will never say, 'Well, that was a bit stupid!' I will always try to come from the place of 'Thank you for telling me. That was really brave. Let's work it out.'

There also have to be some boundaries within my home. Nobody is allowed to smoke in our house, PERIOD. I really don't want my children to smoke. My sister died of lung cancer, and it would really upset me. I'm pretty sure they're all going to try it but they sure as hell can't smoke here. But can I stop them smoking? No. Did I smoke? Yeah. I stopped in the end because I was twenty-four and I realised that I'd given up drugs and drinking but I was still committing suicide. It seemed like the weirdest thing.

Smoking weed, taking drugs – can't do it in the house. That's self-protection as much as anything else. But can I stop them from doing it elsewhere? I can't. I've just got to hope that me talking to them about my experiences, and telling them all that I'm in recovery, will make them think twice.

It doesn't mean you're a bad person if your child goes off the rails. It wasn't a reflection on my dad or my stepmum or my granny when I did. It was just me. I was responsible for my actions. I'm pretty sure my dad felt bad in some way, but now I hope he understands. I think my French side didn't help. In France there were no boundaries. I was allowed to do anything I wanted, wherever I wanted and nobody said anything. So I went nuts.

What will I do if my kids go off the rails like I did? I've got no idea. I'm putting one foot in front of the other. I'm doing the best I can like anybody else. Have I done the perfect job? No! I'm sure there's going to be stuff they think I did wrong.

There will also be things they haven't told me. When I was twenty-four, I confessed to my parents some of the stuff I used to get up to as a teen, when I'd told them I was staying with a friend but actually I was at a rave in a field. I'm expecting all of that.

When they go out, they'll know that I'll always have my phone by the bed and that they can call me any time, day or night. I say to them, 'I'll come and get you, wherever you are. You can call me, 24/7. I don't care what state you're in . . . just call me. I'll come and get you.'

Be a mum, not a best friend

This lesson is something I learned through my relationship with my mother, and I think it is very important.

My mum was often upset. During my childhood and adolescence, I learned a variety of techniques to placate and reassure her, depending on what sort of state she was in.

Sometimes she'd want me to party with her, although I always kept a subtle eye on her to try and stop her from going too far. Sometimes she'd be absolutely furious with something, in which case I would turn into the angel child, absolutely perfect in every way, and love her and nurture her and compliment her into a good mood. Sometimes, if she was insecure and scared, I'd become very confident and funny to make her feel safe. Normally, one or other of my techniques would jolly her up; that is, until my French grandfather, Pasha, died.

When I went to visit her for his funeral, nothing I did cheered her up and, I think, it was because the buck stopped with her for the first time in her life. Her dad had died and she couldn't defer to him. Her mum was around but she was very sad and ill herself. She died six months after my grandfather. Suddenly, my mother had to grow up. There was no one to pick up the pieces, no one to accept the consequences of her wild behaviour except herself. She didn't quite know how to deal with that and I had no idea how to either. This wasn't a situation I'd ever been in before and I didn't know how to make it better.

I think it was then that I realised how much I had always tried to mummy my mum, and that, in turn, made me realise how little she had mothered me. My mother felt like she was losing something when she saw me dressing up and going out, and she had to look better than me, or borrow my stuff and look amazing, because she was so frightened of losing that side of herself. At a time when normally she'd have been going out and having a great time, she had a baby, so perhaps she also wanted to make up for lost time.

Now, when I see my daughter going out, I'm so proud of her. There's not one bit of me that feels jealous, literally not one bit, which I know is not how my mother felt.

I really respect my kids and in return I hope to earn their respect. I don't treat them like little adults, I don't want to be their best friend. Their best friend is their age. I want to be the person they turn to if they need something, or some support, or they're having a bit of a tough time. That's what being a parent is to me. Not being a best friend. I think I'm acutely aware of that because of my mum's need to be my best friend when I didn't want her to be; I wanted her to be Angela Lansbury (you know, wearing a twinset in *Murder, She Wrote*. I bet Angela Lansbury could look after me *and* solve a murder at the same time! EPIC!).

I'm conscious of the line between me mucking about with the kids, loving their gang, yet not trying to be *in* it. I dance like a mummy next to them at a gig, but I don't want to *be* them, I want to be *looking after* them. I think that they like the feeling of safety. Hopefully, they feel quite grounded when they know their mum is on it and she is still there protecting them, even though she's having quite a good time (#justinbieber!).

Sometimes, one of my kids will say, 'You're like my best friend.' I love that, but I always say to them, 'You've got lots of friends who'll be your best friend, and I love the fact that we're great mates, but I always want to be your mummy. I don't want you to ever feel like you have to mother me. I just want to be your mummy if you need me to look after you.'

*

Never say no to a teenager

Katie, who gave me such brilliant advice when my kids were little, also gave me the best piece of advice about teenagers.

I called her up when my eldest was about twelve.

'Katie, it's looming. I need some advice. I'm terrified. Everybody keeps telling me it's going to be the worst thing ever. What do I do?!'

'This one's even easier than the last one,' she said.

'Stop it! Love and boundaries was so easy – to remember anyway, if not always to practise.'

'This is just one thing. Never say no to a teenager.'

'Eh? That is impossible! What happens if they come down in an outrageous outfit or insist on staying out till two o'clock in the morning? You've got to say no at some point.'

Katie explained that teenagers are at the stage in their life when they need some autonomy. They need to feel that they are master of their own universe. We need to show them that *they* are responsible for themselves and we're just there to guide them. If they say something and in your head you're going, 'Over my dead body,' what you actually need to say is: 'All right, let's sit down and you can tell me why you want to do that. Tell me how you think I'm going to feel about it and why.'

'Often,' Katie said, 'you'll come to a compromise where you'll feel like you've given a bit and won a bit and they'll feel the same, which is better than you just saying, "No, my word is the last word," because they're going to baulk at that.'

Anyway, I have used that advice with my children and it has worked out very well. My children teach me things on a daily basis about how much more responsible they are than I give them credit for. How, when faced with a decision, if I give them the space to make that decision themselves, they generally make the one that I would have made.

One of them asked me about getting a second piercing in one ear the other day and I said, 'It just doesn't feel right for me at the moment. Maybe when you're sixteen.' She negotiated me down to this summer, when she'll be turning fifteen, but she had a really good argument for it and as I had mine at maybe fifteen or sixteen I didn't really have a leg to stand on. Then when she asks for something like a curfew time that I feel is too late, I'll say, 'Will you work with me on that?' and she's willing to because I have been flexible with her.

Never throw parties for fifteen-to-seventeen-year-olds!

I've been given some amazing advice by other mums, and also by the kids' schools, about parties and safety. Also, Tanya Byron wrote an amazing article about parenting teens that I cut out and stuck on the board by my computer. I want to be nice, I want to be easy-going and fun, but I still don't let them go to a party if I haven't spoken to the parents. God, I used to hate it when my stepmum did that. It was really, really embarrassing, and even now I find it a BIT embarrassing to do it, but I ALWAYS MAKE THE CALL!

My amazing friend Miriam gave me an ace piece of advice: throw your fourteen-year-old a birthday party and then don't have another one till they're eighteen, because the years in between are the ones when kids are experimenting with booze and smuggling it in in their pants and bras, or filling Coke cans with vodka and lemonade bottles with gin. I think they're right because a) I quite like my house and don't want it covered in vomit, and b) The idea of being responsible for a bunch of really fun fifteen- and sixteen-year-olds, rampaging tipsy round my house just scares the bejesus out of me. So I have offered a daytime party, with twenty guests, not sixty. A garden party, a barbecue, everybody leaves at four – that's fine – and absolutely no sleepovers until they are at least twenty-five . . . Joking aside, I would say . . . eighteen? (I'm still learning too.)

I will never forget my own fifteenth birthday party. I was really tipsy even before it started because a friend had smuggled in some alcohol. My parents had insisted on being in the house and I was SO embarrassed about it. The doorbell went and six boys were on our doorstep. I had no idea who they were. I've never been so thankful to have my dad right behind me. He asked me if I knew them and I just said no and stumbled away, certain my dad could tell I was drunk. He got rid of those boys and I was so grateful. If my dad hadn't been there I'd have been in seriously big trouble.

It was an evening party and there was this boy there who

was gorgeous. He was so hot, I fancied him rotten, but I knew I didn't stand a hope in hell that he'd ever go out with me. There were so many gorgeous girls there. I got this amazing present for my birthday, a stereo with speakers, and I thought it was really cool to put them on the window sill of my bedroom, so we could have music inside and outside the house. Anyway, halfway through the party this really, really hot boy that I fancied so much said, 'Davina, can I have a word with you?'

'Yeah,' I said, trying to look cool but nearly passing out with surprise.

He took me by the hand and led me into my bedroom.

'Holy mother of God, this is the best birthday ever!' I was thinking. 'He's going to kiss me! Hot boy is going to kiss me!'

He got me into my bedroom and shut the door behind us.

'Oh my God, it's all happening! Ker-ching! Best birthday ever!'

He put his hands on my shoulders and he leaned over and I almost puckered up. I was ready for the kiss.

'I'm really sorry, Davina,' he said. 'I knocked your speakers out of the window.'

If there'd been a sound effect to go with that moment, it would have been a needle sliding across a record. IT WAS CRUSHING. The speakers were both really badly dented. On top of that, I think they'd fallen out when he was up there snogging another girl.

*

Saying no with grace

How do you say no without people hating you or ridiculing you?

For example: you're going to a party and your really close friend asks to borrow the dress that you were going to wear. You want to wear that dress but you end up letting her wear it because you don't know how to say no. She looks amazing at the party and you're really upset and feel totally under-confident. That's a huge lesson, isn't it?

I've said this before, but the best way to say no is with humour, or at least a smile and a chuckle.

'You've got to be kidding! I'm not lending you that dress, it's my *favourite*! *I'm* wearing that tonight.' That's kind of funny. It's light.

'Can you send me a picture of your boobs?' 'Do you know what? You're going to have to know me a hell of a lot better than you know me now before you get anything like that. Ha ha ha, lols!' Not, 'Oh my God, what do I do? He won't like me any more if I don't . . .'

Saying no can be very empowering, and it needn't be embarrassing or seem rude if it's done with grace, humour and a huge smile, so nobody will get upset, embarrassed, hurt or ashamed. Sexting is basically modern-day flirting, a sort of foreplay, *but* with the internet and social media, one innocent picture can end up everywhere. I think half the time the people asking for compromising pictures are just having a go. They're thinking, 'I wonder if this one will.'

I had an amazing conversation with the girls about that recently. If boys ask you for stuff, how do you say no without making them angry? I suggested that it's better to make somebody laugh, not make them feel stupid or disgusting for asking. You can't blame boys or girls. They're trying it out, and somebody might say yes. Knowing how to say no is a good tool. Or what if somebody asks you out and you don't want to go out with them? Say no in a gentle way so they're not going to be hurt, because if you hurt somebody, they might act out or they might do or say something mean about you.

Saying no to sex is a bit different. When you are thirteen or fourteen and you're with a boy, don't even get into a situation where sex could happen. If you are lying together on a bed and you know that his parents are out, then things can get out of hand quite easily. Saying no becomes a bit harder because things are already happening.

'Shall we go to my room?' he says.

'No.' Say it then, before you have to say no to the sex a bit later on.

You don't have to be a comedian. Just a smile, a bit of sass, that's how you get 'no' across without anybody feeling embarrassed or angry.

The worst thing in the world is for a girl to feel pressured. I think sometimes boys just want some fun, but then fun can turn into pressure, and boys don't mean to do it, they're just wondering how far they can take it. Once you've said yes, they're like, 'Oh great, she said yes.' It's not a question of 'Oh,

I hope she really means that, I hope she's okay,' because they're not wired like that. It's not their fault, they just aren't thinking that way. So you really have to teach girls to be insistent and steadfast in their decision, whatever it is. 'No' is 'no'. Sometimes 'yes' might change to 'no'. That's still 'no'. It's never a grey area. Right up until the last minute, however frustrating that might be, 'no' is always 'no'.

If you're a parent and there are a couple of fourteen-year-olds alone in a room, go in every ten minutes.

'Can I make you a cup of tea? Do you guys want anything? Supper's ready.' Constant interruption is good!

Don't let kids drink

I know that everybody feels differently about this, but I was partly brought up in France where it is par for the course that children are given watered-down wine from nine or ten, and wine from thirteen or fourteen. I was given a tiny glass of red wine with lunch from the age of twelve, or perhaps even younger, but only when I was in France, never in England.

Until about four or five years ago, it was often thought that this Continental way of giving kids a little bit of wine when they're young, teaching them how to drink responsibly, was preventing binge-drinking in those countries. My experience of family life does not bear this out as both my mother and her brother had a problem with alcohol. They have shown in tests that children given alcohol early are more likely to have a problem with drinking in later life. If you look on the NHS website about children drinking it is quite clear:

> Children and young people are advised not to drink alcohol before the age of 18. Alcohol use during the teenage years is related to a wide range of health and social problems. However, if children do drink alcohol underage, it shouldn't be until they are at least 15 ... Drinking alcohol can damage a child's health, even if they're 15 or older. It can affect the normal development of vital organs and, functions including the brain, liver, bones and hormones. Beginning to drink before age 14 is associated with increased health risks, including alcohol-related injuries, involvement in violence, and suicidal thoughts and attempts. Drinking at an early age is also associated with risky behaviour, such as violence, having more sexual partners, pregnancy, using drugs, employment problems and drink driving.

I do not let my kids drink at all. Obviously, with my history, I'm probably more uptight about it than some people, but a lot of my friends who are quite laid-back parents feel the same way.

I never drank responsibly when I was younger. Never. From twelve I was not just drinking a little glass of red with lunch but was doing any kind of 'party' drinking I could, like slammers, sculling, down in one, wahey! ... Quite laddish drinking. That was me. I wholeheartedly agree with the advice that's given by the NHS and I won't be offering my kids alcohol in my house until they're sixteen. If they drink outside the house in the company of an adult after sixteen, fine, but I don't want them drinking before that at all.

How to have family time

I don't know about you, but the scourge of my family is social media and electronics. If we just left our family to its own devices, Matthew would be on his iPad whilst watching ultimate fighting on the telly; I'd be on the computer in the kitchen compulsively checking the *Mail* online, or working; Chester would be watching football vloggers; Tilly would be watching Zoella and Alfie, and Holly would be on her phone catching up on TV, all in separate rooms. I've talked to friends of mine and I am not alone in this.

So what we do at the weekends is have a family 'appointment' when we sit down and watch the programmes we all enjoy, like *The Voice*, *The X Factor*, *Britain's Got Talent*.

We also sit down at the dining table every evening and eat a meal (unless Matthew or I are working), and I always cook a Sunday roast. If I'm working on a Sunday (which for any future employers that might be reading this book: don't make me do that, I hate it, Sundays are sacrosanct), I'll do the Sunday roast on Saturday. Can I just blow my own trumpet for one moment? I'm really good at it. Chicken, or pork loin with masses of crackling, and for my little vegetarian I do a nut roast.

*

Feeding a family when they all
want different things

I really feel that I am responsible for my children's eating habits. What they eat at home isn't down to them. It's up to me. I am responsible for what I put on the table. This is where I get to parent my children, by what I put in their mouths. This is how I look after them. I do still let them have sweets – I'm not perfect – but they don't have puddings at home unless it's a weekend and I've done one for a dinner party. No puddings, no baking and no sweet stuff. You don't have to have something sweet at the end of every meal, and we train our kids to want that if we give it to them. We're setting up their taste buds for the future.

I follow the French way of cooking and eating. When I stayed in Paris with my grandparents, Maria was the cook, and she made amazing, huge, three-course meals twice a day. That taught me to love and respect food and to understand how much joy we can get from incredible food; how healthy and wonderful fresh, home-made food is.

The French have also taught me to feed my kids whatever I am eating, and that they will like it. I read somewhere a long time ago (and it may have been absolute poppycock) that if you eat something twenty-five times you will like it. I don't dumb meals down for my kids. If you look at a French state-school meal plan for a week, you'll be amazed at the variety of foods kids eat there. Steak, sautéd potatoes, tomatoes, salad, bread, kiwi, fennel, chicory, seeds, chicken casserole, new potatoes, cucumber with herbs, tarte, brie, always cheese with your bread, mushrooms, fresh salads full of colour, onions, courgettes, saucisson, curry, rice, vegetables of every variety. French kids know all the different types of cheeses and all the different types of salad by the time they're twelve. They've had all of it. The French are very proud of their food and it's incredibly important to them. They would rather spend a hundred euros on a meal than a hundred euros on something for their house. In this country we're very house-proud but we don't spend a lot of money on our food.

So let kids eat what you eat. My kids eat salami, spelt, lentils, olives ... Start that as soon as the kids start eating and they'll just eat everything you eat. They try it. If you make your kids spaghetti Bolognese or bangers and mash or macaroni cheese or chicken goujons and chips every day, they're never going to want anything else, because that's what they know.

What I do, if they don't like something, is say, 'Don't worry, I'll make you a sandwich after,' but they have to stay at the table because often they'll try a little bit and actually like it. That happens a lot. So don't just take the plate away. Leave it there, finish the meal and then say, 'Right, what sandwich would you like?' because they might try to eat the meal if they see everybody else eating it. Even if you haven't fed your family this way since birth, don't worry, your kids will get there. It's a bit of a rude awakening but, in the end, kids adapt. I remember when I changed everything to brown – bread, pasta, rice and so on – one of my kids didn't like brown pasta, because it wasn't as nice then as it is now, it was chewy, but she liked it in the end. Now (and I never thought we'd get there because for a long time white bread was the big treat in our house), the kids would choose brown bread over white.

As for catering for a vegetarian, that's been a real eye-opener. Such an education for me . . . We have all, as a family, developed a much more vegetarian palate.

6

How to Stay Yourself (When You're the Breadwinner, Mum, Wife, Sister, Carer, Etc.)

Gratitude

You'll notice that several themes recur throughout this book – one of which is gratitude. When I was trying to get clean, I think it was a sense of gratitude that kept me off drugs. I was so grateful for my dry pillows. I used to sweat so much at night when I was using that my pillows would be wringing wet when I woke up.

Waking up with my head on a dry pillow was just the most luxurious thing ever!

I wish there was a way that I could explain to people how to be grateful, because it makes your life so much better. Gratitude lets me enjoy things. Gratitude gives me joy in the smallest things. I know people who have come from very, very hard beginnings and now have so much in their lives but they cannot be grateful and so are miserable. I know other people who are still struggling and still don't have much in their lives, but they're so grateful for what they have that they lead very, very happy lives. Gratitude is at the root of happiness. Gratitude makes you happy because it helps you appreciate things. Isn't that why everybody gets so happy in spring? We all feel really grateful for the little buds that appear on the trees. We know it's a time of hope and that warmth and light are round the corner.

I try and take stock every day and say, 'Okay, let's name three things that I'm grateful for.' Dry pillows are always on my list. It is such a luxury to wake up on a dry pillow. I'm so grateful for that.

Waking up in daylight is amazing as well. When I was partying, in the winter I'd wake up and wouldn't be sure if it was day or night. 'Is it three o'clock in the afternoon and it's dark, or three o'clock in the morning and it's dark?' I would think. 'I've got no idea, I've been asleep for so long.'

Health. So many people around me are getting sick or less mobile. I'm very grateful for my health.

If I think about all the things I'm grateful for, I realise that nothing else really matters.

Making a list of three things every day that you're grateful for is a great start. It can be the food on your plate, or the roof over your head. You'll get into the habit of reminding yourself to be grateful. Now it comes as second nature to me. I don't even have to remind myself. I just am grateful, for everything. See the tips on page 84 about other ways to develop an 'attitude of gratitude'!

The journey to feeling happy with your body

Feeling happy with your body is a really tough one and such a personal journey. I was quite happy with my body until I got to around twenty-six and stopped clubbing the whole time and quit smoking. I put on about a stone and couldn't shift it. I realised that I had to exercise in order to stay fit. Now I prefer to feel and look athletic than not, but other people might not feel like me.

As I've got older I feel more comfortable in my skin. I look at photos of when I was twenty-two and I looked amazing. I had a beautiful body. I was hot! But did I feel like that then? No, not really. Now I do think I look good, despite the little jelly belly from having three kids. Things aren't as tight as they used to be and my boobs aren't in the same position or as full, but I love my body more than I did back then because working out and leading a healthy lifestyle makes me respect my body and all it's been through.

After my Sport Relief challenge, when I ran, cycled and swam the length of the country, I *really* loved my body. I was so grateful to it for pulling it out of the bag. In the same respect, if I eat a ton of sugar, I'm doing something bad for myself. When I cook a lovely healthy meal I know I'm doing myself a favour so I enjoy it even more. It makes the whole experience of eating and food so pleasurable.

Giving up sugar took me ages on and off, and that's why I wrote the book 5 *Weeks to Sugar Free*, because I needed it myself. In particular I wanted recipes for puddings because, when I had dinner parties, I kept falling off the wagon. I'd make these amazing apple crumbles with tons of sugar, or banoffee pie or a mousse. Now the puddings I make use honey or maple syrup and are free from refined sugar, so I feel like I've stayed on the wagon if I eat them! But they are still meant to be a treat! Just because they are free from refined sugar doesn't mean you can have them every day!

I'm in a good place physically and emotionally when I lead a healthier lifestyle, by which I mean I eat sensibly, I exercise at least three times a week and I manage the level of stress I'm under. I have the odd splurge but most of the time I'm pretty good. That's where I've found my happy place and it might work for you too.

Beauty tips no one tells you about

I doubt very much that my husband will read this book so, on that assumption, I'm going to share a beauty tip with you that I have kept secret from him during our eighteen years of marriage. Matthew still doesn't know that I bleach my moustache. I've tried threading and all of the other ways of getting rid of hair but now I just bleach it. I do it once every two months. It takes ten minutes and I either lock him out of the bathroom or I do it when I'm away for the night in a hotel. I've kept it a secret from Matthew because I think there are some things that he doesn't need to know about. My moustache is only tiny, but when you've got dark hair it shows and it's really annoying.

In my mission to be hairless I went to the beauticians near where I live to get my eyebrows threaded, because I think they look amazing when you thread them. The beautician asked me if I'd like my upper lip done at the same time and I thought, 'Oh Jesus, it must be really visible!' So I agreed, but told her I was meeting Matthew for lunch so it couldn't show. She swore blind it wouldn't and went ahead and threaded my 'tache. Anyway, I walked out with a bright red raw strip of angry skin above my top lip! I had to go into my local where I know literally everybody, with my hand over my mouth. When I took my hand away Matthew literally gasped.

'Aaah, oh my God, what is that?!' he cried. 'What have you done?'

'I've had my top lip threaded,' I admitted, so embarrassed.

'Why? You haven't got any hair.'

'If you only knew what I do to make you think I don't have any hair on my top lip,' I thought.

'I know, I don't know why I did it – and it really hurts,' I said.

He was very sweet but it felt like some little part of my mysterious beauty had been robbed from me, him knowing I have a 'tache. I hope he's forgotten now. So do not thread your upper lip! It hurts like hell and if you have lines on your upper lip I think it makes them look worse.

Modern society has set us women up for a lifetime of miserable hair removal. Even using a laser does not have permanent results and is without doubt quite the most painful thing I have ever experienced. When I did my lady garden with a laser, I thought I was going to put a handprint into the metal bed I was lying on, I was in so much pain.

'Forget it! Forget it! STOP, STOP, STOP, STOP!' I cried. I got rid of the bits that were literally sticking out of my bikini but I couldn't do any more. Part of me also thought that I have a responsibility to my daughters for them not to think that looking normal is a bad thing. Having no hair down there might be OK for some people, but it's actually a bit odd. It makes you look like a child. It's become an immensely contentious issue, to have or not to have pubic hair, and it's a personal journey, but whatever you decide to do, if it's a bit of pruning or a full Brazilian, use hot wax. I always, always, always use hot wax now. For years and years I suffered with strip wax, which they rip off your skin with great painfulness! Hot wax is just rolled off the skin, taking your pubic hair with it, almost painlessly. My cousin introduced me to the joys of hot wax and I thought, 'I'm forty-three, and you're only telling me about it now?' Why are we women not telling each other these things?

This is what the solidarity of women should be all about. Tell me about the flipping menopause and tell me about the hot wax. For the love of God! Don't make me suffer with strip wax for years! And all beauticians out there, don't let a woman strip wax her vagina.

And if you decide just to leave your lady garden to grow in peace, that's fine too. Hair removal is brutal and painful and a woman should never be ashamed of her hair and feel she has to go hairless down there. Girls in porn don't have pubes and boys watch porn, they always have, they always will – but now porn is so readily available, and it ranges from softcore to some really awful stuff, all at the click of a button. The women in porn often have bodies that are only achievable with drastic work: fake boobs, hairless everywhere except their heads; weird hairless creatures. It's not reality and boys need to be brought up to know that that's not real. Boys who watch porn will have an expectation that girls' parts, girls' bodies will look like these unachievable, hairless creatures . . . and that's why it's important for me to look normal, so my children look at me and think, 'Well, Mummy looks like that so it's fine.'

What I've learned through having children is that I am their example. I want to have the kind of body that looks lovely and natural. I look after myself. I make sure I'm fit and healthy and those are some of the best examples I can set. I don't want to constantly change because I'm not happy in my own skin, which is why I haven't had plastic surgery (yet! LOLS). I considered a boob job after I'd had three children but then I thought, 'My kids are going to see that I've had a boob job and I don't want them to feel like they should have a boob job.' I'm always thinking about being a role model to my children and I take that really seriously. The other thing about human grooming is that I just don't have the time. Who's got the time to spend an hour or two hours at the beautician every week getting primped and preened?

There's a very funny anecdote about that. I had gone natural over the winter, and wasn't coiffed in that area, if you know what I mean, when I did an opening link for *Big Brother*, in a shortish dress standing on some steps. A member of the paparazzi took a picture up my skirt and the *Star* put it on their front cover with a picture of a beaver's head over the top of my vagina. The headline said, 'If you want to see Davina's furry beaver, text blah-blah-blah.' Readers could pay £1.50 to see a picture of my pubic hair sticking out of the side of my pants. A friend of mine rang to tell me about it.

'Please don't tell me you did,' I said.

'Of course I did!' he said.

From that day on, I have never had an off-day with the bikini fur.

Being brave

While I was in labour with Chester, I got into the birthing pool when I was close to delivering. The rushes were pretty intense by that stage and I was really in the zone, when Holly walked in and said, 'Mummy, can I stay at home? I really want to see the baby.'

'Of course you can,' I said.

She took off her school uniform, to stop it getting too wet

from the birthing pool, and hung out in those big pants kids wear when they're little, stroking my hair.

'Holly's here,' I was thinking. 'I've got to keep it together because she is going to remember this for the rest of her life. The way that I am right now will shape the way that she views childbirth for ever.' I'd get a rush (as we fans of Ina May Gaskin like to call them,), they were so intense, but I didn't make a sound except a kind of low mooing. All the time she was stroking my hair and tucking it behind my ear.

I discovered a reservoir of braveness within me that I never knew existed, that I now know I can tap into whenever I need to.

I am definitely not braver than other people: I think we all have this well of strength. When I really need to, I can access it; I have it and you have it too. When I was giving birth to Chester, my priority was helping Holly have a beautiful experience to remember, and afterwards it was the thing that I was most proud of to do with the birth – that Holly made me brave.

I think the time I had to pull it out of the bag more than I've ever had to was on my Sport Relief challenge. I achieved things that week that I look back on now and feel were superhuman.

When I was told what I would be doing for Sport Relief, I just started crying. I was totally convinced that I couldn't do seven days of hard, physical exercise. I'd made up my mind before I'd even started. It would involve strenuous exertion for twelve or thirteen hours a day, in February, away from home. I normally do three hours a week max. I'm a mother. I am not an endurance athlete. I have never done a marathon. I don't want to do a marathon.

I sat there, sobbing, and my trainer Greg Whyte, looked at me.

'My job is to build you up so that you are ready to do this challenge,' he said. 'While I'm doing that, at some point, your fear will turn to confidence. I can't tell you exactly when it will happen, but it will.'

'It's not, I'm gonna die,' I thought. 'It's a nightmare. I've got three children. What am I doing? Why am I doing this?'

At the beginning of the training, I honestly thought that I was going to die. We started with 'Workout Wednesday' and between sessions I faithfully followed every single exercise he asked me to do. It was incredibly demanding of my time, and it meant that I saw much less of my family. Matthew was unbelievably understanding, even though he had *the* most horrific news on my first day of training. He was told that his beloved father, Ian, had a terminal brain tumour. Just when Matthew needed me, I had to up my training to include weekends.

'I feel selfish but I'm doing this for Sport Relief, I'm doing it for a bigger picture, and it's only for three months, then everything will go back to normal,' I thought.

Greg literally carried me through the week of Sport Relief, the hardest week of my life. He taught me how powerful it is to have somebody believe in you.

*I don't always believe I can do something, but other
people sometimes believe in me enough for both of us,
and I now try to do that for other people, especially for
my kids. I just believe in them enough for both of us.*

I learned that from Greg. It's making me emotional just
thinking about it. I would walk over hot coals for that man. He
got me through that week and he was always cheerful. He is
truly inspirational.

On day three of the challenge, Leon, my bodyguard, had
to pull me out of Lake Windermere after I'd swum across it. I
had become hypothermic and had to be brought round and
warmed up very slowly over two hours. I was shaking uncon-
trollably for about half an hour. I couldn't speak and was only
allowed to get into a bath after an hour, once my core tem-
perature had risen a little bit. Later that day I climbed on a
bike and cycled a really gruelling sixty miles. And at the end of
it I was quite chipper! I was amazing (no ... I really surprised
myself!). Greg's belief had rubbed off on me, just like he said it
would.

It's lovely to be able to say that about yourself, that you
were amazing. If I'd never challenged myself, never put myself
in a position where I had to be strong, then I would never know
this about myself. There are lots of things that I don't like
about myself but these moments of strength are things I **do**
like. My body and my character are split into bits that I like
and bits that I don't like. It's the bits that I like, the nice me,
that shape my self-esteem. As long as the bits I like are bigger

than the other bits, it's fine. Having people in my life who have believed in me, like Greg Whyte, like Matthew, like my midwife Pam Wilde, like my dad, has made all the difference.

Friendship

I've talked a lot about my best friend, Sarah (aka Sozzlepots). Our friendship is so strong that we don't have to be in touch with each other all the time. We might not speak for a week and then talk on the phone for two hours, or we might speak every day but not see each other for a month. We still feel connected.

Everybody's different, and I'm one of those people who has one best friend and a lot of great mates, but I know people who have six great mates and not one best friend, or others with thousands of friends.

Friends are sometimes the first thing that get neglected when you are super busy but they are actually the people who are going to see you through the really dark times. So don't abandon your friends. Even if you just send a text: 'Hi, thinking of you.' It's important.

Please, please don't be one of those friends who gets really annoyed when your friend falls madly in love and disappears off the face of the earth. When somebody falls madly in love, you've got to let them fall off the face of the earth, because that's the really good bit, the honeymoon period, and then it's over after two years and you slip into the drudgery of normal life where you get pissed off if your husband leaves his plate in the sink and doesn't put it in the dishwasher ... So just let them enjoy. Don't be one of those mates who goes, 'Oh, you've fallen in love and now you don't talk to me any more.' Don't be such a misery-guts! Just let your friend enjoy having rampant sex every day and not wanting to talk to anybody else, ever. I'm giving total permission to all of my friends (and I hope my children would give total permission to all of their friends as they get older) to drop me like a hot brick the minute they fall in love with somebody. In fact, I'm happy to be dropped like a hot brick when they fall in love. Love is great and that really mad, sizzling, smoking-hot passion is so short-lived that you've just got to make the most of it while it's there. Do it, drop me, I don't care.

Complementary medicine

Scientists say that homeopathy is a load of twaddle. Its worth has been disputed for years and years but I've got a deal with my friend Miriam, who's an amazing homeopath, that she treats our family and I give her clothes. She has definitely helped me. I used to get chest infection after chest infection every year and now I don't. I'm pretty sure it's because I'm not pumping myself full of antibiotics every time winter comes. I treat it homoeopathically and it goes away. When the chips are down, wouldn't you just try anything to help yourself feel better?

I've done acupuncture and that helped with muscle pain, and reiki gave me a general sense of well-being. I used to think that reiki couldn't do much, but I changed my mind when I met a woman in New Zealand, I think she was called Anna. She gave me reiki and picked up that I was pregnant, even though I didn't think I was. I would have been about five days pregnant, how amazing? I cried and released a lot of pent-up emotion. When I left I wasn't quite sure what had happened or how it had happened but it felt restorative.

I learned how to do reiki when I was pregnant with Holly so I could do it on myself and on my dog, Rosie, who had osteo-arthritis and absolutely loved it. I've done it on friends too. When Sozzlepots was pregnant she hadn't slept for days. When I gave her a reiki session, she fell asleep halfway through for two hours.

When Chester was born, he had terrible allergies. He only had a 20 per cent chance of getting better and I threw all manner of complementary treatments at him … and he got better. I know he had a 20 per cent chance of getting better anyway, but that's also an 80 per cent chance of never ridding himself of his allergies. Who's to say that the complementary approach didn't work?

The funny thing is, I don't even know if I really believe in complementary medicine and therapies, but I still use them because I think that even if there's a little bit of something in it, then that's a good thing. What I do know is that there is definitely something in energy, in human energy, in a connection with people, in that moment when you meet somebody and you never want to leave their side because they give off something amazing.

I probably wouldn't rely 100 per cent on complementary medicine if I was really sick, but I think it can complement modern medicine in a really great way. Since I've stopped taking drugs and lead a cleaner life, I try to avoid prescription and over-the-counter medicines, and complementary techniques and homeopathy help me to do that. So, I stay open-minded to the possibilities of complementary approaches to health.

The code of the female

I'm not sure if I ever nicked anybody's boyfriend when I was younger than eighteen, but if I did, I'm really, really sorry. I never have since. I think women should uphold a code that we will never nick each other's husbands. It should be set in stone. If it is a *coup de foudre* on both sides, then at least just split up with your partners and give it six months to a year before you embark on anything. It's the law of womanhood. We've got to trust each other. I had an issue with trusting my mum and so trust is the most important thing in the world to me.

There are women who I know to be quite lovely, but I would not trust them with my husband as far as I could throw them. That's such a shame because we need each other. I feel sorry for women who can't be trusted because they're losing out on an enormous chunk of female solidarity.

Mummy guilt

Before I had children I'd planned to go back to work within three or four months of giving birth. I thought I'd be absolutely fine. Actually, I couldn't bear the idea of leaving them and cried every day for three weeks before I started working again. It was just awful. The advice that I get from my mummy friends is that my girls will probably have to work one day so it's good that they see me working, and there was a recent report from Harvard that showed the daughters of working mothers were paid more and took on more executive roles in the workplace.

Even so, it doesn't stop the guilt. Mummy guilt's a funny one because we all suffer it and there's no lesson that I've learned from it. I wish I had a wand that could just magic it away. The best way I've found to deal with it is to share it with my girlfriends. I have yet to meet a mother who doesn't have mummy guilt. Even the mothers who do that 'Oh, I work and I've got a husband and a happy family and we've got it all' – it's rubbish. Even they feel a bit guilty, because there's something terrible about knowing your kid is sick but you can't be there, or missing the play or the match or the choir practice. There are certain things in the calendar that I will absolutely book out for, but there are other things that I can't go to and I feel really bad about that. My kids are really understanding. Talking to other working mums always makes me feel better, because we all feel the same and it helps knowing I am not alone.

Real life juggling

People often mention my phenomenal energy, but it's not always something I'm grateful for. Sometimes, this drive to keep going is exhausting and I really want somebody to say, 'It's okay, stop, sit down, let me make you a cup of tea.' Our nanny, Britta, who has been my friend for ten years and is like a big sister to the kids – we just love her – she's the one person in the world who can make me do that. I don't even let my stepmum or my dad do it. They will come down and give me a hand, but I feel guilty if they say, 'Stop, let us,' because I think, 'No, I should be looking after you.'

I think part of it comes from living with Pippy. She was the person who kept everything together; she juggled all the balls and kept the whole family in touch with each other. I've definitely taken on that mantle. I love keeping my cousins close to me; family is everything! I work, I have my own children, but it's a lot. Sometimes I think, 'Oh my God, I can't do it, I can't breathe.' That's where my fifteen-minute walk without a phone comes in – it's a lifesaver – or Britta will tell me to go and sit by the window and she will bring me a cup of tea. I hope with Britta and me that it's reciprocal, and that I look after her in the same way. It's a mutual love, in a very lovely, feminine way.

Sometimes, keeping all the plates spinning doesn't come from 'I can do it all and aren't I amazing,' it comes from a feeling that I am duty-bound to look after everybody all the time. Sometimes that's exhausting. On the other hand, I absolutely blooming love it and would I have anybody else organise a birthday lunch for a good friend? No. I want to do it. I *want* it at my house. I *like* looking after people. I've got a horrible, horrible FOMO (fear of missing out). I can't bear it if I'm not in on everything. So I battle that as well.

I do juggle a lot of balls and I have got lots of energy, and most of the time the fun I'm having is my fuel. So when it's all great and everybody's happy and I'm making meals and it's all going really well, that's like fuel, because you're just having the best time ever and this is what memories are made of. My kids will love these memories of always having their family round them, of us being close, and being with Pippy, and how lovely all of that is. That's when I'm at my most harmonious. If I can sneak in the odd fifteen-minute walk without a phone I'm fine.

When the wheels come off is when something happens or somebody's unhappy or ill or I'm ill, and then it all goes pear-shaped very rapidly. I think/hope that's normal, it's real life and everybody goes through it, and it's important that other people know that I don't sail through life effortlessly all the time. Who does? Anybody who says they do just wants to make other people feel inadequate.

Take Instagram, for example – that's a brilliant way to make people feel inadequate! The other day I posted a picture of myself wearing some new outfits I've designed with Tesco. I'm really proud of the sportswear I do with them. A friend commented on the post, 'Oh babe, I really love you but I think you've got too skinny.'

'I really appreciate what you said, it's really sweet,' I replied. 'I've just got to explain that I took seventeen pictures and picked the one I looked the thinnest in. I'm ten stone and a size 10–12 so I'm anything but skinny. I show stuff on Instagram that I want you to see. The stuff you don't see on Instagram is me face-planting my daughter's Galaxy egg on Easter Day and dying of a sugar coma, or me and Matthew first thing in the morning. In fact, scratch that, just me first thing in the morning because Matthew always looks delicious.' All the real stuff. And that *is* real and I do the same stuff as everybody else. I have bad moments too.

I think it's dangerous telling people, 'I juggle all these balls and I spin all these plates and I'm brilliant at it and I have a wild sex life and the perfect marriage and three kids who are amazing.' It's not like that. I'd like you to think it is. I want to look lovely and happy and content, but sometimes it's not like that. Most of the time I'm really happy, but sometimes I'm not, that's true life.

*

Accept help

My grandmother Pippy taught me how to be an independent woman. She was very hands-on and did many of the chores that, in those days, would have been considered 'men's work'. She was incredibly capable and taught me how to be capable too, and I really appreciate that; but because of it I find it very difficult to accept help. Any kind of help. For years I would carry all my bags because I thought I should be able to and, as a feminist, I didn't need a man to help me.

I have learned that, if someone offers to carry my bags, accepting help is not weakness.

I *always* offer to help mummies at the airport when they've got a pushchair and five bags and a nappy bag.

'No, no, I'm fine,' they usually say.

'Please let me help you,' I reply.

'I'm fine,' they often say. Then they're fine, I don't insist! But I do think, 'Why do we do that? Why do we find it so hard to accept help?'

I've sought help all through my life. When I didn't feel I could talk to my friends about something, or to my stepmum or my dad, I knew that there was always external help somewhere. It doesn't have to cost money. There are self-help groups everywhere, many run on a similar basis to AA or NA meetings, and they are unbelievably powerful and helpful. You're never alone.

You might think, 'Bloomin' self-help groups and coun-selling, what use is that?' Just try it and if you don't like it don't do it. But once you've tried it and it's worked, then you can see that getting a little bit of help sometimes is no biggie.

Find true peace at Disney

I was in Wagamama the other day with my daughter and a friend from school. This girl is from China and I wanted to give her a lovely experience, but I was trying a bit too hard to be fun and young.

'What's wrong with you?' my kids started saying. 'Who is this woman?' I began to giggle and then completely lost it to the point where people at other tables were laughing at my laughing. Then the kids lost it and we were all in hysterics. IT FELT SO GOOD!

This has made me realise something about growing older. The good thing about it is that you don't sweat the small stuff like you did when you were younger. Things like body confi-dence, confidence in general, relationship problems, generally not knowing what to do – all that stuff gets better. But at the same time I have a propensity to get really serious (#boring). In striving to be a responsible and productive member of society and a responsible and productive parent, I forget that part of me that is nuts, the part that loves to flash her boobs, the part that plays really, really loud house music.

So how do you create an environment where you can feel carefree enough to laugh and let your hair down?

Well, just as my husband has a man cave, I'm making myself a 'she shed' where I can play my music really loud and go mad. It's going to be in the cellar, sound-proofed, and it will be AWESOME. At least twice a year I'm going to go clubbing, because extremely loud dance music is an amazing way to let rip in a way that's not going to get me arrested. I've sort of squished that side of me for a bit, I've put a lid on the wild me, but I need to rekindle her because she makes me feel alive and laugh and feel happy.

I've realised that I need to take every opportunity to be in touch with my inner child because it makes me feel FAB. I discovered this concept big time at Disney. We've gone there every other year since the kids were one and three. When I'm there I am the most embarrassing mother ever known. I put on the Mickey Mouse ears, I've got the Disney lanyard round my neck covered in badges, I go on all the baby rides. I regress. I'm probably at my happiest and most carefree there, because it's okay in those places to really embrace your inner kid and get excited about rides, cartoon characters, musicals and parades. I keep my ears on the whole time while the kids take theirs off after the first day or two.

I don't exactly know why Disney does it for me. I grew up almost as an only child, surrounded by people much older than me, and we just didn't do theme parks and things like that. In adult life, I am quite serious in my job, I have to be on it and concentrate, and then being a parent is also a huge responsibility. Our family dynamic is that Matthew's very funny and silly and does all the funny, silly stuff and I'm the one being responsible and bringing up the rear. When I'm at home I almost forget how to be carefree and silly, but being at Disney allows me to stop being responsible and be a kid with everybody else. I can totally let go. In fact, in a way, my children parent me. I'm begging to go on a ride again and they're saying, 'No, come on, we've got to get round because we've got the other thing to do later,' and Matthew becomes the sensible parent, because he's not as into it as I am. I just go mad and I love that feeling. Sometimes I find that feeling with Soz out clubbing, or if I'm with Matthew without the kids and we go out in London. It's really, really important that I keep doing that because otherwise I might turn into a really rather boring, serious person . . . I might go a bit grey.

When the kids were little, toddlers, I got really sensible and into having routines because otherwise everybody got tired and grouchy and I'd find that really hard. I got quite rigid. By the time we had our third child, I was in a much better space. I knew what I was doing and was a bit more relaxed, but I still feel I have to be careful not to get too sensible. My naughty streak that I need to acknowledge and enjoy often tells me to embarrass my children by singing along to the *Little Mermaid* show at Disney, dancing like no one's watching. I go to that show every single time I'm there. The whole family can recite it verbatim. The children don't want to go any more but they do it for me.

'Please, this is Mummy's fifteen minutes. You *are* coming with me.'

I sing through the entire thing and always, halfway through, I turn to the kids and say, 'Mummy could do better than that.' I'm forty-eight years old and there's some gorgeous twenty-year-old on stage singing her heart out, but I always say, 'Mummy would be a much better Ariel.'

OMG, I just love it so much. There's a sign on the kitchen blackboard that says 'The Dalai mummy finds true peace at Disney' beside a drawing of Mickey's ears. I could write a book on how to do Disney. *Davina's Guide to Disney*.

So, note to self: Don't lose yourself in sensible mothering.

I did for a while. I lost myself and Disney helped me find myself again.

P.S. I've never been paid by Disney. I've never been fast-tracked round Disney. I've never got anything free from Disney. I really do just love it! This is genuine.

P.P.S. As the kids get older Universal is also part of our care-free pilgrimage.

Travelling light

Oh my God, I'm so good at this.

I pride myself on being low maintenance, and one of the ways that I prove that is the small size of my suitcase. I am really, really uptight about my packing. I get very, very annoyed if, at the end of a holiday or a business or work trip, there's something in my case that hasn't been worn. It means I've been inefficient.

To travel light properly takes massive preparation.

1. You need to find out first and foremost the climate and weather forecast for your destination for the duration of your visit. Don't look at it and think, 'Oh, well, it says it'll rain on two days, but it won't.' Take a mac.

2. Shoes take up tons of room so take a pair that can cross over outfits. I lay out outfits before I pack. Things like trousers I'll try and wear two or three times, but I always assume that I'll mess up one pair so I need enough to last me. I'll have a different top every day.

3. Take a comfy nightie. I take my really 'nana' nightie when I go away without Matthew because he won't let me wear it at home. He says it's the most unattractive, granny thing and makes me look 105. It's made of that stretchy material and makes my boobs look like they're round my waist. It is the most unflattering thing ever – it is, I agree with him – but it's soooo comfy and I love it, so I wear it when I go away. I wave it in his face as I pack it in the suitcase.

4. Always take flip-flops. They take up no room. I ridiculously didn't take a pair to Costa Rica when I was filming there. I thought we were just going to be trekking so I only took trekking boots, and I really missed not being able to get my feet out of the boots and into a pair of flip-flops. You never know when you'll need flip-flops.

5. Spongebag – I decant everything into squeezy silicone bottles from the chemist. They are soft and small so I can get millions of them in, it's brilliant. The only thing I don't decant is toothpaste. I don't like any of the mini ones either (I only like Oral B Pro-Expert. It's amazing), but I buy the kids mini ones if we're going away for a few days.

6. Find out what you'll be doing, day and evening, so you have the right outfits but as few as possible.

7. Take enough pants so that you can wear two pairs a day if necessary. Sometimes I'll work out in the morning and I don't want to wear pants that I've worked out in after my shower. I want to put a clean pair on. They don't take up much room.

8. If I'm feeling really flush, I'll do a clothes wash before I go back home so that all the stuff in my suitcase is clean, which is really nice, but that doesn't happen very often because most hotels charge the absolute earth. I think hotels should offer a suitcase wash as part of the deal before you go home.

I'm equally strict with the children's packing. If there's something that's not been worn on the trip then I'm annoyed and the next time they will have to justify packing it.

'You didn't wear that last time. You did not wear that!'

'But, Mum, I really want to take it.'

'Nope! It's not coming.'

So I'm raising children who are as uptight as me about packing.

There was a very funny and rather sad film with George Clooney, *Up in the Air*. His character travels constantly, and he's got the gold Hertz card and the executive platinum American Airlines card and he knows which queue is the quickest to stand in because he travels all the time. He has an affair with another frequent-flyer and then finds out she's married. It's heartbreaking. But I get a bit like that (not the affair with the married woman). I know where to sit in all the airports, where to get the best cup of tea, where are the quietest loos. There's real joy when you feel like you've beaten the system! (Oh God, I've just read this back. I've got to get a life!)

Start being selfish sometimes

Obviously being selfish is not generally a good thing, but what I mean is putting myself before my kids, husband, dogs, once every few months. Normally I put myself last in line and sometimes I need to say, 'You know what? I want to do this and I'm afraid you're all going to have to put yourselves out for me today.' I *never* do that! It feels like a crime. If I'm not working I feel that anything that's not with the kids or not with my husband is being too selfish. I used to go away with Sarah every year for three days but we haven't done it for a couple of years. I've really got to start doing that again because it makes my heart sing.

Sometimes I need a mental health top-up-day, when I spend most of the day doing what I want. It happens once in a blue moon, but I know it makes me a better person. Other times, Matthew and I need time away from the kids for the sake of our relationship. Without our relationship, our children would be very sad. Next week, Matthew and I are going away for three days without the kids. I will feel guilty about being away from them – it feels selfish – but I know that we'll come back and the kids will say, 'Oh, Mum and Dad, get a room!' We'll be embarrassingly loved up, but they'll be happy that we are good together.

When the kids were toddlers I found it really hard because they didn't process it like that. They just thought, 'Mummy and Daddy are leaving us for three whole days,' which to them seemed like an eternity; but even so, we still went away sometimes because it was the thing that kept Matthew and me together.

If you can't get away, go out for supper at least once a week. Go out for a walk at least once a week. Do something just the two of you. Ask a family member to help out with babysitting. Sometimes, being selfish is the least selfish thing you can do.

Stop following the rules

I am unbelievably compliant. In my local town there's a cinema complex with a no-through road that cars aren't allowed to drive down except for deliveries. You could cross anywhere on the road because there are literally no cars EVER, but I always walk way up the road to the pedestrian crossing and Matthew is like, 'Seriously?' I'm so compliant. Anybody else out there like that? I need to rebel against that level of compliancy! Just stop it. I tell myself that a lot.

I'm the queen of giving things up ... sugar, dumb carbs ... but at the same time sometimes I must do something out of the ordinary, naughty, funny – not at other people's expense, not illegal, because I'll get myself into trouble, but just to a point where I feel a bit alive and laugh. Yeah, maybe even cross an empty road not at the pedestrian crossing. Woooooo-hoooooo!

I hate the way I'm so compliant. We were at a race the other day at school, a cross-country race, and a lady from the school had told me to stay behind a barrier. My husband saw six other parents go to the other side to get a much better view of the children, so he just went under the barrier and walked over to the place where he wasn't supposed to be standing. I spent the whole race behind the barrier because I'd been told to, wishing I was with Matthew. Being compliant like that keeps you out of trouble in certain situations, but it also stops you seeing your kid close-up during a race.

Dinner parties

My grandmother Pippy was a master entertainer and taught me that entertaining doesn't have to be silver-service posh five-course meals; it's just about getting together with friends.

I have lots of dinner parties because I love seeing my mates, but I don't stress about the food. The other day there were going to be eight of us for dinner. I had something in the oven but got sidetracked by a child and burnt the dinner. I just called up my friends and I told them we were having scrambled eggs and salmon, avocado and a small bowl of salad for dinner because I'd burnt everything else. They were fine about it.

The trick for a successful dinner party is to handpick a really good group of mates who you think are all going to get on. I love, love, love, LOVE introducing people to each other. To have friends of mine meet and then become friends themselves makes me really happy. I like being a friend facilitator.

Pippy taught me that all the frills, the bells and the whistles are irrelevant, it's all about the company. I'll normally have ten to fourteen people, simple but delicious food, and then we sit in front of the fire and listen to loud music and dance a bit and are silly until the kids come down and tell us to turn it down!

Let it go

Somebody gave me a book about the art of cleaning, which I still haven't read, but I know that it talks about *cleansing* your house and your drawers and everything. I'm a bit torn on this one. I quite like having a slightly chaotic house that feels lived in, but having a clear-out feels good too, like a fresh start. And I'm not just talking about clothes.

Whenever I get a spare moment – and this might sound ridiculous – I cull my Facebook page and my phone contacts. I know there's a weird security in having the telephone number of somebody you haven't seen for nine years, but really, you don't need it and you can let it go. Clothes too: the size-eight jeans from when I was twenty-three. I'm never going to get back into those. Let them go.

The leather coat I bought from Jigsaw thirty years ago that's upstairs in my cupboard. It's got to go. That leather coat is never coming back in. EVER.

I have ooh-aah boxes for all the interesting stuff the kids do, but I go through them every few months. I keep two or three works of art from each era, but I don't keep everything. When they were young I felt awful throwing away anything of theirs, but actually I can't keep all of their art, it's too much. They do absolutely tons of it. Pick out the best stuff, or the stuff that you think they'll like the most, and keep that. Be brutal.

It's hard to maintain that of course. When you're really busy do you want to spend your whole weekend just decluttering? But you need to do it if you don't want to feel like you're drowning in stuff.

There's a reason why it's called 'spring-cleaning'. It's because spring is the season when you get that amazing feeling of a new start, a change, new buds on the trees, fresh air, early mornings, breathing in through your nose and out through your mouth, filling your lungs, positivity, maybe just a T-shirt outside, and spring-cleaning makes you feel like that – even if you do it in winter. There's a wonderful purging feeling, like when you take the Christmas decs down – you get a bit depressed for a minute but then you have a good clean and think, 'Oh, this is good! This is good!' New year, new you, fresh start. We need that.

Kids hate change, so I have to purge their clothes on the quiet. Sometimes I tell Chester that his favourite pyjamas from when he was six, or the trousers that are way too short, got chewed by the dog.

Of course, there are some things that I will keep for ever. I have a drawer full of birthday cards that my kids have made for me. Chester wrote me one that said: 'Mum, you are hawt for your ag.' I'd told him once that it was nice to pay people compliments. It was so sweet. I'll be pulling that one out at his wedding.

Sometimes, it's emotions we need to get rid of. Resentment is a big one. It's toxic. It makes us sick and keeps us down.

I've had somebody tell me that they were angry with me about something that had happened three years earlier. I wasn't even aware that I'd done anything. We resolved it right away, but they'd had all this anger inside for all that time. I'm sure that holding on to that kind of stuff makes you sick.

I have learned to tell people as soon as possible if they've done something that I'm upset about, because chances are they have no idea, but I'll be getting more and more angry and frustrated. With one conversation I can completely get it out of the way. It usually goes something like this;

'You know what happened this morning? I feel really upset about it.'

'Really? But why?'

'Because it made me feel like blah-blah-blah.'

'I didn't mean it like that at all!'

'Oh really?'

'No!'

'OK. Thank you.'

End of. Seriously . . . often it really is THAT simple. Letting something fester is the worst, worst thing. Get rid of it. Offload. Move on.

Unplug

The other day I went for a walk and didn't take my phone with me – it was brilliant. So simple. Don't take your phone everywhere. Look up. There's a whole world happening and we've forgotten that. My best and most creative ideas always come when I haven't got my phone with me, because if I *have* got my phone with me I'm constantly checking my social media and the *Daily Mail* website, which is like crack cocaine.

I know that mindfulness and meditating are good for me. It doesn't really come naturally to me though, so I have learned how thanks to an app called Headspace. It's brilliant. You get a ten-minute guided meditation every day, and it's not hippy-dippy or religious, so everybody can do it. It was created by Andy Puddicombe, who has taken what he learned from being a Buddhist monk to help with modern-day mindfulness. He is a genius.

If I'm using the app, and especially if I'm away somewhere, I do sometimes manage to meditate and be mindful, but the reality is that I'm just not very good at it. At stopping. So, for me, just going out for a fifteen-minute walk without a phone is also stillness.

Silliness is good for the soul

My dad taught me the art of being silly and I've made a career out of it. I've definitely passed it on to one of my children, my oldest, and I think my other two are developing a really good aptitude for it. I like skipping – I'm forty-eight. I like dancing. I like doing things that someone my age definitely, probably shouldn't do. The other day (and this is a 'high-class' thing to do because I've got a swimming pool), nobody was in so I took off all my clothes and dive-bombed into the swimming pool. It was brilliant fun and I felt so naughty! I want more of that, please.

Silliness can get you out of a multitude of problems and is a very valuable tool against feeling insecure or awkward. If you act silly it makes you seem confident and less bothered about what other people think of you. My dad was always really silly. He was forever sticking runner beans up his nostrils or pulling silly faces to make me laugh. He's legendary for tying his tie around his head and dancing like Mick Jagger. At his sixty-fifth birthday at least ten people told me he'd done that at their wedding. Depending on the level of alcohol consumption, he'd sometimes take his shirt off as well, for a treat.

He taught me not to take myself too seriously and that's such a valuable lesson. Making a fool of yourself takes practice, and it will be painful while you practise because you have to really throw yourself into it, and if you're awkward it will have the exact opposite effect to the one you want. It's the idea of dancing like no one's watching: you just have to let go of all self-consciousness.

I think my dad got his sense of fun from Pippy. She was always mowing the lawn in her petticoat, she didn't care if the postman came, and would make fishy faces at mealtimes and sing songs. Carefree silliness really is food for the soul.

Let's talk menopause!! (Well, someone's got to)

The menopause is something we just don't talk about and I don't really understand why. When I was in my mid-forties and it started happening to me I thought, 'What the bloody hell is this?' Women don't talk about it. I think it's associated with drying-up ovaries and becoming old and on the shelf in a society where we're all obsessed with youth.

I was in Prague doing a shoot for Garnier and I was sweating so badly all night. I was up and down three times wondering if I had flu. Sitting in the make-up chair the next day, I was still boiling.

'Oh my God, is this chair heated?' I asked.

The make-up artist looked at me like, 'You're weird. Of course it's not heated'.

My back was on fire! My whole body was on fire.

After a week or so it died down, although my periods were a bit erratic. For a while everything went back to almost normal, so I didn't talk to anybody about it because I just thought it was a weird week. I was forty-four. The menopause just wasn't on my agenda.

Then it happened again a few months later and somebody said, 'I think it's the perimenopause.' I was getting night sweats a couple of times a month and would be up and down and up and down. I wasn't sleeping; my keys were in the fridge, my phone was in the bin, I was struggling to read autocue, I couldn't concentrate on anything. The kids and I would just be leaving the house and one of them would ask, 'Have you got my hockey socks?' I would go, 'WHY HAVEN'T YOU GOT YOUR HOCKEY SOCKS? WHY ARE YOU ASKING ME THAT RIGHT NOW? WHY DIDN'T YOU ASK ME LAST NIGHT? FOR THE LOVE OF GOD! YOU'VE GOT TO SORT OUT YOUR OWN STUFF!' Then I'd get in the car and all the way to school I'd hate myself. I spent my whole time apologising to my family for screaming at them. Matthew talked to his friends about it; he clearly thought I was going a bit mad. My libido went all weird, because the night sweats made me feel so unsexy and uncomfortable and I was just exhausted.

It all came to a head when I did my Sport Relief challenge. I was cycling, swimming or running 500 miles from Edinburgh to London, and I got my period on the first day and had night sweats every night. I thought I was having a nervous break-down. It was the most insane week of my life. I decided after that that something had to give!

I went to see the gyny and he told me that I was definitely perimenopausal and talked to me about HRT. My big worry was an increased risk of cancer so I looked into bioidentical hormones, which a lot of people talk about as being a natural form of hormones, but they haven't been widely studied. I was told I've got something like a forty-five in a thousand chance of developing cancer anyway, and I think with HRT it's forty-seven in a thousand. It's a totally personal decision and I did the research I needed to make decisions I'm happy with.

I was really helped by a book, *The Wisdom of Menopause* by Dr Christiane Northrup. This is the menopause bible. It's the *What to Expect When You're Expecting* of menopause, the *Road Less Travelled* of mid-life, and it was like the author was talking to me personally. The first page made me cry and cry and cry and cry and cry:

> My love and concern for [the children's] welfare usually overrode any anger or frustration I might have felt.
>
> But as I approached menopause, I found myself unable to tolerate distractions such as my eighteen-year-old asking me, 'When is dinner?' when she could see I was busy ... Why couldn't my husband get the dinner preparations started? Why did my family seem to be almost totally paralyzed when it came to preparing a meal? Why did they all wait in the kitchen, as though

unable to set the table or pour a glass of water, until I came into the room and my mere presence announced, 'Mom's here. Now we get to eat'?

I mean, yes! I love this woman. A word of warning before reading this book: if your marriage is a little bit rocky and you've been all menopausal, don't read it and think, 'I need to leave my husband and go and marry somebody else,' which is what the author did. A common side effect of the menopause is a relationship crisis, but you don't *have* to get a divorce! Therapy can work a treat too!

I want to tell everybody reading my book to get *The Wisdom of Menopause* (obvs not if you're twenty) because it tells you everything you need to know. Dr Christiane Northrup isn't massively into HRT but she informs you about it, and also about tons of other ways of coping with more natural methods.

The very valuable lesson I learned from it is that the menopause is a life-changer. Once you've got over the fact that it means that you won't have any more children – and I did grieve the loss of that possibility.

<u>It's the dawn of a new era in your life.</u> No, seriously, trust me, it is.

I feel really excited about moving forward into a stage of my life where I'm not the bottom person on the totem pole. I've moved myself up the pole and can now say, 'Guys, I can't do that actually because I'm doing something for myself.' SHOCK HORROR!

The other day I'd been away, working all weekend, which I try to never do, and it had been mega-stressful. I so wanted to pick the kids up from school on the Monday but I also really, really, really needed to sleep. I was self-indulgent and thought, 'My husband works *but I also work*. Why is that I have to be the one who rushes like a maniac to pick up the kids?' So Matthew picked them up and it felt to me like an exciting, utterly selfish act, that I would never have done ten years ago when the kids were little. Afterwards I apologised to my son that I hadn't picked him up and he was totally fine. I think they see that I put myself out for them most of the time, so they really don't mind if I do something for me. In fact, they're happy for me. Possibly I should have been thinking a little bit more like that throughout my whole life, but it was important to me, given my own upbringing, that I give my children a lot. Now, I want my daughters to see that I'm making myself important too.

I always thought that I would retire at fifty but I'll be fifty next year and far from wanting to retire, the menopause has made me want to turn into some sort of crazy businesswoman! I've got renewed energy and more vim and vigour than I had when the kids were toddlers, because I was *so* exhausted the whole time. Now I'm really fired up about work and where I'm going and what I'm doing. It's a new horizon. There's an attitude that menopausal women are past our sell-by date and are unattractive and unworthy of love or self-love. In fact, it's the opposite! I'm feeling more minxy and überlike the older I get.

*

Don't be a moaner

I did a programme called *On the Couch with Big Brother* where we had psychologists and therapists breaking down the behaviour of the housemates. It was brilliant. I learned so many interesting things, one of which was about moaning.

For example, people who moan about turning up in fancy dress to a fancy-dress party – that's 'status-boosting moaning'. Basically they're saying, 'Oh God, it's so stupid getting dressed up for a fancy-dress party.' It's moaning about something that everybody was quite looking forward to doing but because someone's moaning about it they feel embarrassed to be enjoying it so they start moaning too! Status-boosting moaning makes people feel stupid for wanting to take part in something, to boost the status of the moaner.

I used to think that moaning was quite useful because you offload your woes, you get them all out, you share and let them go. But there's sharing and then there's moaning.

Now I know *that moaning is futile.*

It doesn't make you feel better. It doesn't make the person you're moaning to feel better. It just makes everybody feel rubbish.

I was working with somebody I hadn't worked with before and they were moaning about everything. It was depressing! I was thinking, 'Today could have been really lovely ...' but this person was moaning about literally everything: the lunch, the situation, exhaustion, the weather. We were all in the same boat and I just thought, 'God, this moaning is making everything hard work.' There was nothing we could do to change it, we all just had to get through the day together. Like whining, it's attention-seeking. Children do the same thing. Sometimes people moan because they want sympathy. Actually, moaning makes you want to walk in the other direction very fast, or tap them on the shoulder and say, 'Oh well, jolly on, chin up, trot on, socks up!' Know what I mean? Come on! Moaning is really insipid.

Ina May Gaskin, queen of all things birth-related, has given some amazing tips for life in general, including on moaning. She said: 'Don't complain, it makes things worse. If you usually complain, practice not doing it during pregnancy. It will build character.' In pregnancy, I think, a lot of women moan because we're just massive and heavy, but Ina made me realise that if I didn't moan and just got on with it, my family and people that I worked with or anybody around me, were happier, and it felt good.

Even when you're ill, moaning is pointless. The kids know that when I'm *really* ill I go to bed. When I've got a cold or a cough, I try really hard not to moan and, in fact, I get a lot more sympathy! Everybody can see I'm not feeling that great and they're really nice to me.

If you've got a genuine problem that you're sharing with a friend, then that's just talking, isn't it? 'God, there's somebody at work who's driving me a bit nuts at the moment . . .' That's a conversation. 'Well, what could you do?' There's a solution. I think with moaning, people don't want a solution, they want attention.

Moaning doesn't change anything for the better and it bloody ruins everyone else's day too! Don't do it. It doesn't get you anywhere, and status-boosting moaning is even worse because it makes you feel holier-than-thou but makes the people around you feel like worthless lumps of caca. It's horrible. So if you're invited to one of my fancy-dress parties, God help you if you don't turn up in fancy dress. You'll be off my non-existent Christmas card list.

It's interesting that moaners are often quite self-aware. 'Oh God, I've got to stop moaning,' they say. 'YES! YOU'VE GOT TO STOP MOANING!' I say. I hope all moaners who read this book will think, 'Oops, that's me. I've got to stop.'

Yes!

Sometimes things are just bad

This is another lesson that Matthew taught me. My husband, even though he's got puppy-like enthusiasm, will often put the brakes on a situation that I'm rushing into. When he's down I can cheer him up; I just put my positive spin on it . . . but there are times when putting a positive spin on events is just not the right thing to do.

I remember when poor Matthew's dad was diagnosed with terminal cancer. Matthew was really upset, of course, and I was trying hard to make it better. I searched so hard to say something that might cheer him up. He looked at me and said, 'Davina, you can't put a positive spin on this. Please stop'.

'Oh my God, I'm so sorry. That's not at all what I was trying to do. Of course I can't put a positive spin on it. Of course, this is terrible. I'm gonna just shut up and give you a hug. Sorry,' I said.

That did teach me that actually sometimes people just want or *need* to feel grief and you can't make everybody better all the time. Even though I want to make everybody happy and everything okay, there are times when something cannot have a positive spin.

Grief

The interesting thing with grief, having gone through it with my sister Caroline and then subsequently with Matthew's dad, is that grief doesn't say, 'Okay, I'm gonna come and visit you for two months after the death and I'll make you feel very sad but then you'll be fine.' It's not like that. There were times after Caroline was cremated that I'd have a fantastic couple of days and almost feel guilty about it, and then other times when I was catatonic. Something very small and unexpected would trigger my grief, like picking up a potato peeler. Caroline and I always peeled the potatoes together on a Sunday. In fact, Sundays hurt for two years. Every Sunday morning I'd just feel so low.

I liken it to being dumped. For the first month, at least, I'd wake up every morning and my first thought was, 'She's gone.' There would be that feeling in the pit of my stomach, that ache. Then I'd get up and start my day and it would be fine. Then a year later something would floor me. I remember doing a round-table interview for *Got to Dance* and one of the journalists was from *Inside Soap*. The poor man said, 'Hi, I'm from *Inside Soap*,' and I burst into tears. Every Tuesday of the last seven weeks of Caroline's life I bought *Inside Soap* for her, because she loved it. I'd read it to her and we'd laugh together. She was cremated with a copy of it (and copies of *TV & Satellite*, *Grazia* and *Closer*) on the top of her coffin. And so grief hits you at moments you don't expect, not just soon after the death but for years. Grief doesn't have a timetable and when it comes, let it wash over you, because there is no way to stop it.

7

Stop Worrying About the Future

Growing old ... disgracefully

We spend a lot of time fearing the future, I think, fearing getting older and mourning the loss of youth, but this fixation with youth is really dangerous. I tell myself to stop worrying about the future and enjoy the day. I spend so much time worrying that I forget to look up, to look down, to see the kind person giving me a smile, to watch flowers coming into bloom, to smell the spring, because I'm thinking, 'Oh my God, tomorrow I've got to get up at six-thirty,' and all that.

I remember realising this as the kids were growing up. I would think, 'I can't wait until she can walk,' 'I can't wait till she's out of nappies,' or 'I can't wait for this,' and then I saw that I wasn't enjoying that one moment when they are sitting in the sink having a bath and how cute that is.

I walked past a café this morning and saw a woman with grey hair having coffee with her friend and they were in hysterics. I thought, 'Oh, you're lovely!' Laughing makes people so attractive. The stresses of being in your twenties, thirties, forties, trying to get ahead at work or be on time or get the kids to school or can you conceive or are you ever going to find a boyfriend? Most of that disappears as you get older, and you have that chance to really laugh, let go, let rip and be naughty. If you're naughty when you're older it's even more shocking, and therefore even more fun.

I was on Twitter the other day and somebody had written 'You shouldn't be posting stuff like that at your age, blah-blah-blah'. I replied: 'Look, I am really sorry but I intend on growing old really disgracefully so if you can't take the heat, unfollow me.' I laughed a lot picturing his face when he got that.

You don't *have* to grow old disgracefully, but my point is that I don't think any of us should worry about what is 'age-appropriate' any more. There's no such thing as age-appropriate. Wear what you want when you want, have your hair how you want. There is no age to go grey. There is no time to stop wearing a bikini. I'll still be wearing a bikini when I am so wrinkly that you'll be able to stretch my stomach from here to the next village. I don't care. If I want a brown tummy, I'm wearing a bikini. I don't want to go topless, but if you want to go topless at eighty, go topless! Do what you want.

It comes back to judging, which I do sometimes but which I don't like. Don't judge other people for the way that they are. I really love the fact that we, as a nation, embrace people who are different. We love female stars like Paloma Faith, who's got such great, individual style, or Lady Gaga or Madonna. Amazing, expressive women. Madonna has always had to put up with people telling her she shouldn't be something or other . . . but she's strutting and stroppy and sexy and doesn't listen to her critics! She is fit as a butcher's dog, out there, still working, a creative person who loves what she does. Good on her! She's doing what she wants to do. I'd like to be as fit as her I hate it when people judge other people for their choices.

My favourite thing in the whole world is when fashion magazines do spreads on OAP fashionistas, women between sixty and eighty who are still smashing it in the fashion stakes (and smashing it in the fashion stakes effectively means wearing a lot of stuff that doesn't really go together but is quite wild, topped with a massive pair of sunglasses and orange hair). That is totally what I'm going to do. I am so going to be an eighty-year-old fashionista, still wearing massive fake-fur coats in a multitude of different colours. I plan to always surprise people with my hair. It will be a never-ending source of shock, and I'm going to dress wholly inappropriately for a woman of my age. I will maintain a youthful spirit and go out clubbing at least twice a year, because that makes me very happy. I'll always listen to really loud music. And laugh a lot. Laughing definitely keeps me feeling young. And I'll never retire. Look at Angela Rippon. She's amazing and totally on it in her seventies. I'll always keep a toe in. If I stop doing TV I'll go straight down to Radio Kent and ask for a middle-of-the-night slot once a week, so I can play loud music. That's what I mean by growing old disgracefully. Don't put an age limit on anything. Don't put up those barriers. *Everything* is open to you for ever.

I don't fear death

My sister taught me how not to fear death. For that I will be eternally grateful. We were unashamedly, unhealthily and gloriously codependent. We both had very complicated relationships with our mum, in different ways: mine in a 'please just mother me' way, and Caroline in a 'please stop trying to be my sister and mother me' way.

My sister was four when my mum met my dad and left her behind in Paris with our French grandparents. My sister and I grew up with similar but slightly different problems. She had more of the traits of an adult child of an alcoholic. She really struggled with relationships. I would put that down to the fact that my mum took a couple of boyfriends off her when Caroline was a teenager. Because of that, my sister had trust issues. Who wouldn't? If you can't trust your mum, who can you trust? She wanted to be loved but was just too frightened to be with anybody in case they were taken from her.

My sister came to live in the UK when she was twenty-five and I was nineteen. We didn't hang out much back then as I was in the midst of profuse partygoing and getting off my trolley. My sister smoked a bit of pot but that was it, so she wasn't a massive fan of my behaviour. Our paths crossed a bit (she used to work with me waitressing sometimes), but when I was twenty-eight or twenty-nine I bought my first flat and she rented the other bedroom off me. We got really close then. I loved it. She was fun and cuddly and motherly and sisterly and very French!

When I met Matthew, the first time I brought him round for a cup of tea to meet Caroline she grilled him. She knew that I was rubbish at choosing men so she wanted to talk to him. Caroline was so protective of me. She crossed her arms and her legs and put on her fiercest Parisian glare! She was very hostile towards him and her line of questioning was extremely fierce. Afterwards she decided that he was a nice guy! But poor him! He was terrified!

As I became more successful, I became more and more protective of her. She wasn't brilliant at managing her finances, and I have been ever since my dad taught me that most valuable financial lesson. So, as I made more money, I realised that I could help her a bit by having her continue to live with us. Matthew was nothing short of amazing because Caroline was living with me when I met him and she just sort of stayed. We bought our first marital home together and she had a room in the attic. She was like his big sister and it worked brilliantly.

When we moved to the country she was determined not to leave London, but four years later she moved into the cottage next door to us. Every weekend we were together; in fact, we spent almost all our time together for about fifteen years. She never married but she had a great job in advertising where she was really popular and had lots of amazing friends. She was a Scorpio, so she trusted people after they'd earned it, but if you put one foot wrong, if you ever did something to hurt her or any of her friends, THAT WAS IT. You were never spoken to again. You were off the Christmas card list. She never forgave. I'd be like, 'Do you think you might ...?' No. *Non, non, non!*

For her fiftieth birthday, which was in November, she had a party and by Christmas I remember saying to her, 'Blimey, Caroline, you've lost so much weight!'

'I know, it's great, isn't it?' she said. During perimenopause, and with an allergy to healthy food and exercise, she had put on a bit of weight around her middle. Losing it made her look really good. We thought she was getting fitter, but in fact she was fostering a really unhealthy Advil addiction for the pain she was in. She didn't tell me this until later.

Then she started withdrawing slightly. She was somebody I saw almost daily, but she stopped coming round so much, which was what used to happen when she had financial problems. I was sure something was amiss. When she did come round she seemed a bit clumsy, but every time she tripped down a step or walked into a door, she'd laugh and say, 'Senior moment, senior moment,' using the menopause as the reason. I thought maybe she was not telling me something. Maybe she was worried and was smoking more pot?

What we didn't know was that she had a brain tumour that was causing her to lose her peripheral vision. The back pain was from lung tumours pressing on her spine.

She smoked 'with impunity' and always said, 'I'm not going to get cancer because my grandfather lived till he was in his eighties and my other grandma too. They all smoked. I'll be fine.' But actually she wasn't.

Lung cancer was what started it all off, but she was asymptomatic except for a cough that she'd had for as long as I could remember.

We went away in the May half-term and had invited her, but she had come down with what we thought was flu. She told me she was going to stay in bed and not go to work. What I didn't know was that two days before we left she'd been fired from her job. She'd made a few catastrophic mistakes and they'd sent her to the office doctor because they thought something weird was going on with her eyes. But the doctor had done something which annoyed Caroline and she'd left. That was very Caroline. She was very French and very stroppy. By then, there was nothing the office doctor could have done anyway. The cancer had already spread to her brain, because it was affecting her eyes.

Even when they'd fired her, she hadn't told me. She would carry stuff like that. When I think about that it makes me very sad. I told her all my woes, and she hid hers. She was very, very secretive – classic adult child of an alcoholic.

So, we went off on holiday and when we came back she was still off work, and still ill, curtains drawn. She told me she'd been to the doctor and he'd given her antibiotics, but she hadn't. She didn't want me to make a fuss. She wasn't like me. I'd have gone straight to the doctor, I'd have made a fuss.

A few days later somebody was walking past her cottage and they heard a cry for help. She'd fallen out of bed that night and she couldn't move. She was paralysed down one side of her body and she'd lain there smoking cigarettes all night, crying. Her phone was in the other room and she couldn't get to it.

I called an ambulance because I thought she'd had a stroke, but the stroke team came and didn't know what it was. They took her into hospital and gave Caroline a brain scan.

'Good, we'll find out what it is,' I was thinking, but when they also took her for a chest scan I couldn't understand what they were doing. If she was paralysed down half her body, surely it must be a stroke? Pippy had had a stroke the week before, and when I sent my dad and cousins texts about Caroline's possible stroke, they all wrote back, 'Don't you mean Pippy?'

Then the doctors started asking her whether she could see their fingers as they wiggled them at the side of her head. She was saying 'No, no, no, no,' and only said yes when they were right in front of her.

'This is really bad,' I was thinking.

They were checking her back, listening to her lungs. In those situations, it's funny the things you remember. One of the things that made me so sad was a big spot on her back that I would have loved to get my hands on.

'Who sees you naked? Who knows you? Who sees your body? Who's looked after you?' I thought. I'd looked after her as best I could, but she never let me see her naked, EVER. She had always suffered such low self-esteem about her body. No one had intimately loved her for a long time, and I felt so, so sad about that.

So many doctors came and went that I think we were both beginning to worry. Finally a doctor came in and said, 'Look, this is serious.' Caroline just said, 'Oh shit.' Then he told us that Caroline had tumours in both lungs and that the cancer had spread to her brain. She had two brain tumours, all inoperable. The next day we discovered that the cancer had also gone into her spine and she was developing bone cancer as well. They gave her eighteen months to start with, then nine, then secretly, to me, they gave her six months. She went in seven weeks.

To start with, they gave her amazing steroids that made her feel radically better. It was great to see her so bubbly.

'I'm feeling amazing, everything's fine' she told everyone who rang, and afterwards they would say to me, 'She sounds so good.'

'No,' I'd say, 'listen to me, this is bad. If you want to come and see her, come and see her.' I felt like the Grim Reaper.

The steroids worked for about four weeks but the cancer was close to her brain stem, and as it spread, bits of her shut down. It was devastating. She went blind and she slowly became physically incapacitated. She was in hospital for a month and we managed to get her back home for the last three weeks. Because she was so bad with money she didn't have a penny, and the NHS helped her so much in those last few weeks. I called her office and told them what had happened, that her sackable offence had been her brain tumours, and they reinstated her on full pay until she passed, which meant so much to Caroline because it allowed her to give some money to her godchildren. It was just an extraordinary, beautiful, beautiful thing.

In those last few weeks, when people were coming to visit, she gave everybody presents. She got us to wrap up various items of clothing and bits of jewellery. She was so giving.

The amazing thing about being with Caroline on that journey was not only witnessing her extraordinary bravery and her absolute courage but seeing how she put other people's feelings above her own. I often saw her being brave for other people because she could see they were really struggling. She would pull it together for **them**. I only hope that I can do that for the people I love when I go. She was selfless. When her friends came round I watched her rally and be amazing. When they'd gone she'd be so tired. She *never* complained. Even when she lost her sight, she just pretended she could still see, but I knew she couldn't because I'd walk in and she wouldn't know I was there until I spoke.

Even in the face of death she gave me this lesson as a present: when you die, you will leave people with memories of the journey of your death for ever, it is part of your legacy. On Caroline's journey, there was something that she did for me that I *know* was a gift. Four days before she died, she was very, very poorly. It was about 6.30 p.m. I had *never* seen her naked. She had seen me naked almost daily; in the evenings I'd call her and say, 'Caroline, I'm having a bath, will you come and chat?' That's when we'd have our debrief. I'd be parading around the bathroom stark bollock naked and wouldn't think twice about it, but I had never seen her with her clothes off – even every summer when she came on holiday with us, she would always have a sarong over her swimming costume.

When she got to the stage where she needed help undressing at night and getting into bed, a hoist would lift her out of her wheelchair and into bed. She had to be covered in Diprobase to prevent bedsores. I could have done it because I took all of that time off work – you know, the world stops, you can't do anything – I was just there, but Caroline really didn't want me to do it because it was her last piece of dignity. She preferred somebody she didn't know seeing her like that. I totally understood but I felt rather sad that the carers got this really intimate time with Caroline. The night before she went to sleep for ever she was so tired and agitated. People with brain tumours often do this knitting-like thing with their hands and Caroline was doing that frantically, saying that she couldn't breathe and wanted to go to bed.

I said, 'Okay, but it's six-thirty and there's only me and Claire here.' Claire was one of Caroline's carers and the most kind, beautiful human being. She put Caroline's dignity above everything else and I owe her the hugest debt of gratitude. She was from Ghana and I bloody loved her. I said to Caroline, 'Me and Claire can put you to bed, but it means that I will be getting you undressed and putting the cream on.' She went, 'Yeah, yeah, yeah. That's fine.' In my head I was thinking, 'OMG! She's going to let me put her to bed!'

So we used the hoist to lower her onto the bed. The lights

were dimmed and all was calm. We undressed her and then she let me cream her. It felt lovely, running the cream up and down her arms. She had always had the softest skin and beautiful long fingers. She must have been able to tell I was really enjoying it, feeling all of her body and taking in every inch of her skin, and when she had to sit up so I could do her back I leaned into her ear and said, 'Thank you, Caroline. Thank you for letting me do this,' and she said, 'Don't get used to it,' in her angry, stroppy, French way, but laughing. At that moment, I couldn't have loved her more.

In a way, I got a chance to mother her in the way that our own mother never did. Maybe that's why she never let anybody look after her, because she hadn't experienced it. I'd been lucky. Pippy did that for me. She was *so* tactile; she saved my life. So did Gaby. Caroline had never had that.

It was unbelievably powerful that Caroline let me do that for her the night before she left, and I *know* she gave that to me. The next day she was really uncomfortable and, for the first time, really frightened. She couldn't swallow any of the pills so I called the doctor and asked for liquid versions of them all. She was on a lot of pills. Pills for blood sugar levels, pills for fitting (she was having seizures), pills for de-swelling her brain ... It was intense the number of pills she was on, and half of them were to stop the side-effects of the other half. The doctor told me that some of the medicine was available as liquid, but the ones to counter side-effects were not. I said, 'So what's going to happen?' He told me she was near the end because of the seizures and the jerkiness. He said he could make her comfortable, ease off her muscles and help her be calm. As she was going to sleep she looked at me and she said, 'I'm scared Mummy.' I said, 'It's all going to be okay'.

She went to sleep very slowly and I pulled a mattress into her bedroom so I could sleep beside her for the next three days with Bo, my dog. On the third day her breathing slightly changed and I woke up immediately. Matthew came running over and Gaby was there as well. Matthew held one of Caroline's hands and I held the other, and her breathing just slowed down, and slowed down, and she passed away peacefully.

The way she handled herself, the way that she helped me and Matthew and all of her friends and our kids get through it, the way that she left us all with a little piece of her, was so inspiring. After she died I realised that I was not scared of dying any more, even though I'd always had such a huge fear of it.

She left a big hole and I know that all her friends would say the same thing. She didn't have kids but we were all her family. She was a consummate birthday-card writer. My friends are lucky if they get a Facebook message. She spent her entire wages in the ribbon shop VV Rouleaux every Christmas, buying the most extraordinary ribbon and wrapping each present with such care, as if it were the only one she was giving. She had so many funny little isms that made me laugh. She'd come on holiday with us with her suitcase only half full of clothes. I'd be amazed she could travel so light, but the other half would be full of two-year-old issues of *Inside Soap*, *Now*,

Closer and *Grazia*, because there were a few articles she hadn't read. Then she would bring them HOME again. Every Tuesday I had to go and buy them all, as soon as they came out. That was why we put some on her coffin, she'd have loved that. She collected frogs, she always wore scarves, she was obsessed with the Royal Family. She used to boss me about a lot, but I loved it. I really loved it. I LOVED HER.

Tips for being a brilliant granny

Now, I know I'm not there yet, but I do think about how I'll be when I'm a granny, probably because I lived with my granny, and my granny looked after my great-grandma. I have learned these lessons from the glorious Pippy – like so many other lessons in my life – not from anything she told me, just from how she is.

1. Be a grateful granny. The thing about Pippy is that whenever I see her, even if it's been five days since my last visit because I've been away filming, she'll always say something like, 'Oh, it's so lovely to see you. Thank you so much for coming. Seeing you puts a spring in my step. You always make me feel so happy.' Is it any wonder that after spending time with my granny I skip out of her cottage feeling loved and cherished? Pippy is such a grateful person. Gratitude, as you know, is one of my favourite things. The fact that I always *want* to go and see my granny, that it's never a

chore, has been an amazing lesson to me. It's because she's a grateful granny.

I'm really determined to be a grateful granny when I grow older.

I've have some friends with really grouchy grannies. The minute they walk through the door their granny is complaining about not being visited enough. This is the quickest route to nobody ever wanting to see you again. I am literally allergic to people trying to make me feel guilty. I don't know what it is from my background, but it makes me want to flee!

2. Don't kiss your grandchildren. This is key if you want to be visited by your family, especially small children: don't try to kiss them. That's a no-no when you're a granny. Let them kiss you but don't swoop down for a smacker. I think they find it a bit frightening.

3. Always have a sweetie jar. Any granny who does not have a sweetie jar is missing a trick. The sweetie jar is sometimes the only reason my kids go to see their great-granny. Chester will zoom over to Pippy's with all of his mates for a flying visit.

   'Hi, Pippy!'

   'Do you want a sweetie?'

   'Yes please.'

   'Here's the sweetie jar.'

   Chester will introduce his friends to Pippy as they're peering into the jar.

'Do you want a sweetie too?' she asks.

'Yes please.'

Then off they shoot again, and she loves it! It's youth. That lovely energy young kids have, it rushes in and washes over her. She feels included and we enjoy having her around because she's so fun. That's the kind of granny I want to be.

Dreams and goals

My dreams and goals for the future are to be near my kids and their kids. I've got a horrible feeling that they're all going to emigrate but that just means that Matthew and I will travel a lot.

My other goal is to have a tiny place in the South of France, on the coast. I see myself writing or walking, with that amazing light, and I see Matthew and me having very lazy French lunches and siestas and the sound of water lapping.

I just want to see my kids and have my place in France where I learn how to knit and be quiet. I've lived an amazing life and have been to a lot of places and I am satisfied. I know lots of people who are never satisfied but after Caroline died I thought about it a lot. Am I satisfied? I am satisfied.

Books I've Found Helpful

Where Willy Went and *More and More Rabbits* by Nicholas Allan. A very sweet and funny way to explain how babies are made.

Mummy Laid an Egg: or where do babies come from? by Babette Cole is brilliant for explaining sex in age-appropriate language.

The Day the Guinea-Pig Talked by Paul Gallico. About the friendship between a little French girl, Cecile, and her guinea-pig, Jean-Pierre. Always had me in tears . . . still does.

Spiritual Midwifery by Ina May Gaskin is literally my bible. My copy is very well thumbed. It's not only good advice for expectant mothers, but in life generally. Here's a taste:

Advice for mothers at the time of birth: Be grateful that you're having a baby, and be grateful to your partner who's helping you – it's an experience that you only do a few times in your life, so make the very most of it, and get your head in a place where you can get as high as possible. Learn how to relax – it's something that requires attention. You may have to put some effort in to gather your attention together enough that you can relax.

Blink: the Power of Thinking Without Thinking by Malcolm Gladwell. Fascinating insights into our subconscious and the ways in which it helps and hinders our thinking and behaviours. It teaches us to trust our instincts.

Outliers by Malcolm Gladwell is also totally enlightening and is where I first read about the need to do something for 10,000 hours to be successful at it.

Linda Goodman's Love Signs by Linda Goodman. When I was dating, I almost wouldn't go out with somebody if we weren't compatible according to Linda Goodman. Even if you don't believe in astrology, this guide is eye-opening about relationships.

Men are from Mars, Women are from Venus by John Gray. There's a reason this book was in the bestseller lists for so long.

How to Be Brilliant by Michael Heppell. How to go from average to brilliant in every area of your life.

How to be a Woman by Caitlin Moran for making me literally laugh and cry so hard.

The Wisdom of Menopause: Creating Physical and Emotional Health During the Change by Dr Christiane Northrup. The bible for menopause; not just the physical symptoms and what you can do about them, but the emotional ones too.

The Road Less Travelled by M. Scott Peck. This book taught me the value of doing the things you don't want to do first, so that you can enjoy the feeling of having done them.

The Happiness Project by Gretchen Rubin. An account of Gretchen Rubin's year-long project to know what 'happiness' meant to her, and how to achieve it. Thought-provoking.

Join Me by Danny Wallace. How doing things for others can make you happy.

Acknowledgements

I would like to thank Matthew, for being very patient with a therapy-loving recovering addict who loves pop music and is enthusiastically positive! Thank you for all the lessons we have learned together – we work.

Thank you to our children, who guide me through parenting, and teach me how to be a better person. You heal me.

Big thanks to all the inspiring people who have taught me the most amazing lessons, in particular I have to mention Pippy, and my Dad.

Thank you to Lucy for helping me edit my rambling words . . . Didn't expect to make a new mate!

God Amanda Harris, what can I say? You are incredible. BTW . . . I'VE GOT ANOTHER IDEA ;-)

Rowan, I love you!

Mary and Emily – the dream team – thank you for making my dreams come true. I love you guys so much!

And thank you Soz, for being my best mate through thick and thin. You are **my person**.

Try **Davina's** recipe-packed healthy cookbooks

Out Now!

Order now at
www.thisisdavina.com/shop